THERE'S MORE TO ME

A STORY OF EXPERIENCING RADICAL SELF-LOVE
AND FORGIVENESS THROUGH A JOURNEY OF
OWNING ONE'S PAST, SHAME, AND LIMITING
BELIEFS.

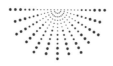

SASKIA ST LOT

SOULFULLY ALIGNED PUBLISHING

ISBN: 978-0-578-31598-0

This book is dedicated to my 19-year self, who was looking for answers and had no idea where to start looking. This is also dedicated to every single woman who is living in the shadows, wanting more for herself but afraid to take the leap. I hope you're inspired to start your own journey and learn to start choosing you every single day. Know this: YOU have been and always will be enough. All you seek is within. You are not alone and you don't have to do this alone.

CONTENTS

PREFACE

You are about to go on a journey. The journey of my life and transformation. I want to express that this book is not a guide to how you should live your life or what you should follow for yourself. I am simply sharing my story with the intention that you get inspired to start living a life that is authentic to you. To step out of the shadows of fear, rejection, shame and doubt and step into your own self-love and self-discovery journey to rediscover yourself. I firmly believe that who you are as a person is perfect as is. There is nothing wrong with you, nothing to change, nothing to fix. You may want different results but it doesn't mean that to get there YOU have to change. Your habits, your mindset, your perspective may have to adapt but who you are at your core is perfect. You are enough. It's what makes you uniquely and unapologetically YOU. You get to go on your own journey to meet you for the first time for who you really are, who you've always been but may not have been ready to accept or embrace.

This book is a vulnerable outlook of my life, my journey, the setbacks, shame, obstacles, triumphs, challenges and lessons along the way. It is my journey back to self. Through this journey, you may encounter parts of my story that may be challenging to read and process but I hope that it challenges you to look at the parts of your story that are challenging for you to accept and process. I hope that you discover and experience: 1) How to own your story and past. 2) Be in full expression and acceptance of self. 3) Find your tribe and build supportive relationships. 4) Learn to forgive and reconnect with yourself.

Before we dive into this journey, I want to first thank those that have made it possible. Abba, thank You for being with me throughout my entire journey, You are my strength when I have none and I am because You are. Moms and Paps, I cannot thank you enough for the sacrifices, support and love you have shown me. No matter what I take on in this life, you always show up for me even when you don't understand or see my vision. You have always supported me and you have taught me what it means to build a family based on love, trust and support. Chaton et Mamsie, je vous adore, merci pour tout le support, l'amour et la motivation.

Sach, you are my rock! Without you, this dream wouldn't be a reality, publishing this book wouldn't have been a possibility. You pushed me and encouraged me to follow my passion and dreams when I didn't believe it was possible and you have stood by my side loving, supporting and growing with me. Thank you for being with me on this journey called life. Thank you for giving me not one but two sisters and thank you for the best gift of all, the two little munchkins that I love so dearly. I couldn't have been blessed with a better brother, You are the best there is.

Lastly, thank you to my coaches over the years, especially my book coach Sandra for helping me get clear on my vision and bring it to life. Thank you for believing in me and taking a chance on me. To my friends and coaching team, you have been my village, you have cheered me on when I was down and when I was celebrating. You have been there every step of this book journey and I am grateful for your love, support, patience, cheerleading and faith. You taught me what it means to be in relationship with others and what it means to ask and receive support.

I love you each dearly.

NEVER THE SAME

Some things happen in one's life that create a rude awakening, let's call mine May 2016. My story doesn't start then but everything in my life began to shift at that time. May was an exciting month, I was graduating high school and it would be my last year in Haiti before going off to college. I was born and raised in Port-Au-Prince, Haiti. Growing up, I always looked forward to being independent, living my own life, and making my own decisions. I couldn't wait to finish high school. I was eager to graduate so that I could leave home and start an independent life.

I had this idea that Haiti was always going to be my home, no matter how much I couldn't wait to leave it, I always felt it would be the place I would come back to settle down when the time came for it. It's where my family was, it's where I grew up and it was all I'd ever really known. I always thought it would be home. At the time, I couldn't even see a possibility where I would have the option to not settle down in Haiti. I would even feel guilty thinking of the option of living abroad, away from my family. Even though Haiti is known as a third-world country, in my mind, it was our reality and it was our home, it was my normal. It's weird to explain but it felt safe to me even during riots and insecurities because, at the end of the day, it was the place I used to call home. In May of 2016, that story began to change.

Graduation week was exciting. As a salutatorian of my class, I had to prepare a speech. Some nights at the dinner table, I would stand up after dinner and rehearse what I had written so far with my mom. I would pretend it was graduation day and I basked in the pride, excitement, and also anxiety that came with giving a speech and graduating. I was proud and I also remember asking the principal if someone else could do it. I couldn't picture myself giving a speech in front of hundreds of people, what would I say, what would I sound like, oh my, I didn't feel qualified. I also remember talking to my friends about our summer plans and what was next for us, we were all so eager and scared at the same time. We would all be embarking on an unknown new path.

As scared and uncertain as I was, this was the moment I had been waiting for my whole life, well almost, I couldn't wait to graduate college either but let's not jump the gun, I hadn't even started college then. As celebratory and memorable as that week should have been, some things took place that changed that for the worst. See, day before graduation, my father was arrested and what was supposed to have been a short meeting with lawyers and judges turned out to be a seven day long nightmare.

In the morning, my mom and I went to the hair salon to get pampered and dolled up for the award ceremony. We were giddy, sassy, and joyful. We couldn't wait for my dad to pick us up so we could get there. I couldn't wait to attend because I knew as a Salutatorian, I would receive graduation stoles, cords and awards and I was ready to bask in the joy and pride of my hard work. While we were at the hair salon, my mom got a phone call and by the look on her face, I already knew something had taken a turn for the worst. She told me my dad was being held by the judge and she was going to take care of it.

I went straight into strategic planning mode, I needed a solution for what I knew would be worrisome and concerning for my mom. As she was taking care of getting my dad released, I took care of transportation from the hair salon to my house and from my house to the award night. I reached out to two friends and in a couple of minutes, I had done damage control. My mom no longer had to worry about my night or how I was going to get there, I had taken care of it. Right now, the only priority was getting my dad back to us.

I don't remember getting home, getting dressed, or getting to school for the ceremony. I arrived at the award ceremony about five-minutes before it started and my mom showed up devastated. She came to me and told me they had arrested my dad and she had no idea how or when they would release him. My mom began to cry so I comforted her and told her that all would be fine. No clue how but I knew we weren't going to give up. The rest of the night was blurry. They say when something is traumatic your brain has a way of blocking the memories to avoid feeling the pain, I make up that's what's happened here. I felt alone, scared, lost, and confused.

That night when I got home, as I sat on the living room floor in the dark, praying and crying, it hit me, everything in our lives was about to change from this point on. I had no idea what it would look like or what it would mean for our family but I knew our lives would never be the same. What was intended to be a simple, celebratory day turned into an unexplainable night. What was happening? Why was it happening now? Why was it happening to us? I didn't know, but I did know we were in for a ride and it was not going to be a smooth one. I cried, letting myself feel the fear of the future, the fear of tomorrow, wondering if he would be released in time for my graduation or would that morning have been the last time I would have seen him for a long time to come? So many questions, uncertainties, and story-making, yet none I made up provided comfort or ease, just angst, and worry. So after a while, when I realized there was nothing for me to do, I got myself together and headed to bed. Tomorrow would be a new day and I needed to make the best out of it. After all, it was my graduation day and I was supposed to be celebrating.

GRADUATION DAY

The day was there, the day I had been waiting for these past six-years. That morning though, I wished I didn't have to go. I wished I didn't have to graduate. Even hoped it would get postponed because I wanted my dad to be there so badly but unfortunately he couldn't. My mom, brother, and family were doing everything they could to have him be there with us, constantly on a call with lawyers but nothing was successful.

Everything was happening so fast and so slowly at the same time. One minute I was at home getting dressed and the next I was in line, getting ready to walk into our graduation ceremony. As I walked in, the first person I saw was my Godfather. He was taking a picture of me as I walked towards the stage and tears began to fill my eyes. "Don't cry, head high, chin up and smile, just smile, people love your smile" that's what I kept repeating to myself as I walked through those doors. My dad is my picture guy, the one who captured every major moment of my life, from my first birthday to our first visits to the zoo, to my dance recitals, he made sure every moment was captured. So not having him be there for such a moment in my life was very hard for me. However, since I had a speech to give, I couldn't allow myself to have any emotions. I needed to be put together and smile, so, I numbed out my emotions and proceeded to walk.

When the time came, I got up from my seat, gave my speech, smiled for the pictures, hugged people, and laughed, pretending it was a typical graduation day and nothing was happening in my life. When in reality, I was in a lot of pain. I wasn't just sad because my dad wasn't there, I was sad because my family was in pain and there was nothing I could do about it. I felt helpless and powerless. I even felt guilty for graduating. I felt like I wasn't allowed to celebrate like I was supposed to be doing something productive but instead there I was taking pictures, laughing, and smiling. It felt wrong. I was so angry, angry at life, angry at God, angry at the whole world. I couldn't understand how they were illegally holding my dad. I couldn't comprehend why we weren't fighting harder, why we were staying quiet and taking things a day at a time. I wanted to revolt, yell and scream but instead, I told myself I had to be strong. I had to be strong for my family and my dad. Now wasn't the time to feel and express, now was the time to stay quiet and be perfect.

JAIL VISITATIONS

The day after graduation, my mom told me that we could visit my dad. The first time I went to visit him in jail, I was numb and afraid. Afraid he would never get out, afraid he wouldn't make it in there, and afraid that the father I knew would be gone if he ever got out. Seeing him behind those blue bars, sorrow engulfed me. I was distraught that I couldn't do anything to help him. I thought of all the things I should've done differently like all the times I should've told him how much I love him and how much of an amazing father he is. All the times I should have thanked him for all he did. I was filled with regret and sorrow as if I would never get the opportunity again.

When I started talking to him behind the bars, two other inmates came up behind him. I was afraid they were going to ask questions I shouldn't answer, I froze a little. See, before going to see my dad, my family had decided that we should pretend to be friends and acquaintances so our identity would remain anonymous and the other inmates wouldn't know who we were. We were afraid of how they would react and treat my dad.

What happened when we got there, I never in a million years expected. When I approached my dad, the two other inmates looked at me, smiled, and started shouting "congratulations!!" They told me they knew I had graduated the day before and they wanted to wish me the best. I didn't know how to take it in. I smiled and thanked them and after a minute or so, I stepped out because I couldn't breathe. I was overwhelmed, it was too much. I didn't know how I was supposed to feel, react or respond. Here I thought we had a plan to not share our identities but there I was with strangers receiving acknowledgments and they already knew who I was before I even said a word; my dad had already shared everything.

It made me feel more guilt as I told myself "If you hadn't graduated yesterday, this experience wouldn't be as hard for him. He wouldn't have the pain of knowing he missed his daughter's graduation." I made up that my graduation was a bad thing because he didn't get to be there.

The next couple of days were foggy, they consisted of jail and court visits, waiting, praying, and hoping. One day, I went to visit my dad and while I was there, a woman came to visit her husband who was in the same cell. She stood right next to me as she began to speak with him. She wanted to know if he had a court date and when he informed her that there hadn't been, she began to cry. I will never forget the look of despair she gave me as she began to cry. He asked her to leave because he couldn't watch her cry. She walked away crying, feeling hopeless and scared. I stepped outside to go find her and told her to stop crying because right now he needed her to be strong, he needed her to believe in him more than anybody else, he needed to know that she would be okay with or without him. As I was telling her this, I was telling myself the same thing to keep me from breaking down. I didn't want my dad to think I was hopeless and despaired, I wanted him to know that we would be fine without him if we had to. The real truth though was that I was a wreck, emotionally, mentally, and physically but I was just doing a better job at hiding it.

After seven days, as they had no evidence to hold him any longer, they released him. The longest seven days of my life. Every time I think about those seven days, I relive these seven days of hell, uncertainty, no answers, frustration, sorrow, and seven days that made absolutely no sense.

At a time in my life where I felt the world should have stopped, it just kept on going and no one was stopping. There was no pause, no rewind, no breaks, just a constant, Go. Go. Go.

It was exhausting, especially pretending to be perfect all the time, so people wouldn't ask more questions or give more sympathetic looks. I was so tired of the pity, "feeling bad for us" energy people would give our family. I just wanted us to go back to normal but what did normal even mean for us anymore?

I hope you never know what it's like to have to pretend to be okay when your entire world feels like it's falling apart. It's heart- wrenching and it's very lonely. As "the real world" continued and a new week began, everyone went back to their daily lives as if nothing had happened and I on the other hand couldn't just go back to our "normal lives". I began to question everything.

Everything I grew up knowing up until that point suddenly didn't make as much sense anymore. My dad who was always supposed to be our rock, protector, and safety net had just had his entire world stripped away from him. The country I had believed and hoped in had become unrecognizable or maybe I was just really seeing it for the first time. The rules and family mottos such as "if you are a good person and do the right things, good things will happen to you" became questionable. The people I expected to show up, be there and support us through that time, all of a sudden were nowhere to be found and I was filled with anger and rage. I was disappointed and hurt. I couldn't understand how I was expected to go back to the life we were living as nothing occurred. I began to wonder, "What is the point of all of this?" What's the point of following all these societal and family "rules" and expectations when "life" happens anyways and at the end of the day you're left with just you?

I had no clue how to process what I had just lived, I did what I knew best, I put on a facade pretending everything was just peachy.

I moved to Miami for University, settled into my new dorm, went to class during the week, and partied over the weekends. I was living my "best life", or, at least, I was trying to convince myself that I was. I had created a new "normal" for myself. The more I put on that mask, the more my defensive walls grew. I saw everyone as a threat or an enemy, someone who would destroy my life. I grew distrustful of everyone and began to trust no one, even family and loved ones. I kept all my relationships superficial and at a distance. It was too scary to allow someone in because the thought of vulnerability terrified me. After what I had experienced, just the idea that allowing someone in could give them the power to hurt me had me disconnect from most of my relationships. I could not handle any more pain, so instead, I surrounded myself with emotional walls and superficiality. Anything but vulnerability and connection, when it was probably the thing I needed the most during that time.

2

MASQUERADE AFFAIR

The second semester of my freshman year syllabus consisted of Margarita Monday, Tequila Tuesday, Wine Wednesday, Grove Thursday, Friday, and Saturdays were reserved for going out to clubs with my Haitian friends and Sunday was recovery and church day. I was out most days of the week and without a doubt every single weekend, no matter what exams or projects I had going on, I was always partying. I wanted a fresh start, a new narrative, and a group of friends I could call family. Anything to bring me pleasure and fun.

I rushed to join Greek life at the beginning of my spring semester. I thought if there was a place I was going to find myself and my tribe, it would be in a sorority. The rushing process was emotionally and physically exhausting. It was perfect for me though because it was what I did e-v-e-r-y-d-a-y : Get dressed, put on a smile, pretend I'm perfect, and talk to people about how great life was. It was all so superficial and inauthentic! I remember going from suite to suite feeling like I was putting on a show every time. Yes, I was "being me" (whatever that meant then), but I was also trying so hard to be liked by everyone. To be honest, I don't even know what was truly me and what was the version of me I thought these girls wanted me to be.

I just wanted to fit in somewhere. I wanted to be liked, I wanted to be cool, I wanted to feel like I belonged. I was trying to make sense of life. Every day we would find out which sorority we got called back to and which ones we didn't. I remember feeling so good because the top-tier sororities kept calling me back every day until the last day. Last day I was left with only one. I couldn't believe that I had been dropped by my two favorite sororities, but I also didn't want to walk away from this experience so I said screw it and I gave it a chance.

I honestly loved it the first semester. I had joined their dance team, we would compete for Greek week, I would go out with them and I always had something to do and people to hang out with. I got along really well with the senior sisters, I felt so connected to them and I finally began to feel like I was starting to belong.

As the year continued, I found myself in a dilemma. I didn't know how to be Catholic and be in a sorority at the same time. I felt like I was living a double life, one foot in one foot out. I would go to church every Sunday and attend Bible study every week but I would go out on some weekdays and weekends and drink every time. While it was fun, it was also exhausting and draining.

I got to a point where I was tired of doing both. I was feeling guilty about going out, drinking, and partying, but when I didn't I felt like I was missing out and being a Debby downer. I couldn't say no to people. It was a mental battle for a couple of months, what do I do? What do I choose? After two to three months of living this life of constant partying and avoiding, I decided to dive deeper into my faith.

As I did that, I began to lose some "friends", as I didn't drink or go out as much as I used to with them. So there I was, right back to not belonging anywhere. I felt like my Catholic friends didn't understand me because I wasn't "Catholic" enough and now my sorority sisters no longer related to me because I was too "Catholic". They no longer felt comfortable around me. I was in a whirlwind of confusion once again.

Burned out, always trying to prove myself, prove that I fit in and that I was enough became overwhelming, so instead of communicating and expressing myself, I chose isolation. It was simpler that way, I didn't have to please anyone and I also didn't have to disappoint anyone.

The more I isolated myself, the more depressed I became craving connection but being terrified of it. Some days I would shut off my phone so I didn't have to connect with anyone and other days I would get out of my bed at 10 PM but only because I needed to pee. Weekends would be spent in bed eating peanut butter and bread because it was the closest item to my bed and getting out of my room was not an option. Skipping class and emailing teachers telling them I was sick, was something I had started doing more frequently. I never dared to say what was going on: depression and anxiety. It wasn't like this every day but the lows were low and the highs were high. I was so ashamed of the way I felt and so afraid to speak about it that on the outside I made it look like I had it all together (are you even surprised at this point?).

During my depressive episodes, I met an angel, Takei. She became my best friend, she lived right next door to me and I basically lived in her room. I could go to her at any time of the day or night and she was always there. The great thing was, we were both avoiding reality so we didn't have to talk about it, we just drank wine, laughed, acted silly, and had a great time. Some nights, when we were both in our lows or I was deep in my lows, I'd pour out my heart, she'd listen and we would just sit there. She was the first friend that I allowed to see me when I was a mess.

With my best friends from home, I was so afraid that if I showed them how broken and depressed I was they would pity me, feel bad for me or judge me. I didn't want to be seen as weak or broken, I wanted them to see me as the life of the party and cheerleader. So with them, I faked it so they wouldn't ask questions and when they got suspicious that something was off, I would back away and disconnect. Being seen was not an option for me, not at that time, I wasn't ready yet.

THE FIRST TASTE OF HEALING

One day, as I was walking to class, I saw the counseling center office and decided to stop by. I walked in, talked to a counselor, and decided I would give it a try. I began to attend counseling every week. My counselor was phenomenal, she met me where I was and walked with me through everything I brought each session. When I first started with her, I didn't believe I needed counseling. I decided to give it a try because

I thought it wouldn't hurt and if anything I could work with her on remembering my childhood since I didn't seem to remember as much as other children. I was always curious as to how children could remember memories from when they were four years old but I couldn't remember anything from those times. I thought maybe I had a memory problem. Maybe she would be able to fix me and tell me how to remember my childhood like everybody else. At that time in my life, I also couldn't express how I felt, I was too afraid to feel my emotions, especially the ones that felt heavy. I would always tell her that I felt like if I started feeling one heavy emotion, I would never stop crying as everything I never dealt with would come back up. I knew that my wounds and pains were deep, so I wasn't ready or willing to go there.

As we began to dive into my past and life, I realized I didn't go to her to remember my childhood, we never really spoke about that because that wasn't why I really went. The more sessions we had, the more I realized I was in therapy to heal. I was there to work and heal the traumas and pain I had not dealt with, such as losing my grandfather to cancer when I was ten years old, losing a loved one in the January 2010 Haiti earthquake, going through my first heartbreak at thirteen years old and more. There was so much I was holding on to and with my dad's arrest, that was the last straw. Subconsciously I knew I needed professional support but I wasn't ready to admit to myself that I was not okay and needed help. Whatever story I told myself that had me walk through those counseling doors, I am eternally grateful because it changed my life. I started to unravel the pain and trauma I had been holding onto for years. Pain I had been holding onto for eight and more years, pain I thought I was over but had never taken the time to process. It was finally catching up to me.

My counselor created a space for me during our sessions where I felt like it was okay to be real, it was okay to admit that I was not okay, it was okay to cry. She showed me what empathy looked like and I got to experience her being with my pain. I got to experience support, not pity. She cried for me when I couldn't cry for myself and she stood with me when I shared my pain and scars. She sat in silence with me when I didn't have the words to speak and she made me feel safe in a world I had become scared of. It was a beautiful partnership and process. It was very painful at times but beautiful because I began to wake up, very slowly but the work of healing had begun.

3

ONE DRINK TOO MANY

*G*rowing up, I always had a goal to save myself for marriage, to save myself for the right one. One reason was that my faith told me to. The other was because the society I grew up in expected women to be chaste. I also felt like it gave me some kind of power. I was able to tell people that I was 18-years-old and still a virgin, and that was rare. Most people didn't believe me, and many were surprised. I had dated men before, and most were way more experienced than I was, so I understood when people questioned me, but it made me feel unique. I had something most women didn't; I was special. I took pride in that fact. It was something I thought no one could take away from me because it was mine, and I had no plan to give it away any time soon. I had left relationships because men wanted me to sleep with them, and I wasn't ready. I was always in control.

When I got to college and began to question everything, I questioned saving sex for marriage. I asked friends around me who had experienced sex before what it was like, and they raved about it. They would talk about how amazing it was and tell me I was missing out. I began to feel like something in my life was missing, like I could have more but wasn't allowing myself to. I was 19-years-old, and everyone around me was supposedly having great sex; I felt alone. I wanted to experience the euphoric high and pleasure they were referencing. I was curious and wanted to fit in.

I was also trying to figure out where sex fits in with my faith. One side of me wanted to have sex, and the other side reminded me that I should wait for marriage, I was Catholic, after all. I battled my faith, questioning why I should wait and why it was so wrong when others claimed it was so great. The internal battle lasted for months.

As I pondered and questioned, I came up with an alternative, a compromise: self-pleasure. It was great in the beginning, but then guilt and shame overcame me. After all, Haitian women and women of faith are taught that anything sexual, especially self-pleasure is wrong and disgusting. So I began to see myself as bad and disgusting. How could I say I was a Catholic yet completely ignore the teachings of my faith. I was confused and tormented.

I slowly began to back away from the church and my faith and decided that I wanted to explore my sexuality more. I wanted to have more intimate experiences, and I wanted to belong. I wanted to have a friend or boyfriend I could explore with, someone I would feel safe to try new things with, someone I cared about, but I was too afraid to ask anyone I knew. It felt weird, shameful, and uncomfortable, so I never reached out or found that friend.

There's a part of me that wants to skip this next part of my story and get to the part where I had great sex, learned to love and heal my past, but that's not why we're here today. Being able to share this story with you and this part of myself, knowing that that girl doesn't run the show anymore, is part of my healing journey. I'm at the choice, and I choose to share this story knowing that I get to choose what defines me and what doesn't.

In November of 2017, I went out to a sorority event and met a guy friend there. We had a great night dancing and even stepped outside to talk. It was the first time I expressed to someone that I was battling faith and sexuality, wanting to save myself for marriage while also wanting to experience other sexual activities. He commended me for still being a virgin and choosing to wait for marriage and even told me that he respected me even more for having that standard for myself. He shared that he wishes he didn't use sex as a way to feel better about his self-esteem but that for him, sex was a way to feel enough and masculine. I was glad to have been able to have such a deep conversation with a guy and not feel ridiculous for choosing to wait.

After my sorority's event, being drunk, I wasn't done partying, so I went to another bar with a girlfriend. I invited him to come as he was interested in that friend, but he couldn't make it, so he asked us to come to his place instead when we were ready to go home. He had ordered pizza, so I thought, why not? She got tired and chose to go home, but I headed over anyway. On my way there, I thought to myself maybe this was the opportunity I had been looking for, that friend I wanted to explore more with, especially since we had had that conversation earlier where he knew I was saving myself for marriage. The worst that could happen was that we would make out, it would be horrible, and it would be awkward between us for a while; so I went.

When I got there, he asked if I wanted to change into comfortable clothes. I was still wearing my dress clothes from earlier that night, so I was relieved to change. As I was undressing, he came over, and we began to kiss. One thing led to another, and we were doing more than kissing, but since I had never done anything before but kiss, I reminded him to be gentle. He began to pleasure me with his hands, but as it was my first time and I had alcohol in my system, it felt uncomfortable, I wasn't aroused. I wasn't quite sure what we were supposed to be doing or how it was supposed to feel. I just thought it shouldn't feel as uncomfortable and painful as it did; after all, we weren't having sex. He realized my discomfort and tried to make it better, but it wasn't working. Being intoxicated and not knowing what to expect, I just laid there, hoping it would feel better at some point. Being the people pleaser I am, I had no idea how to say stop, that it was painful, or to say, "okay, let's not do this anymore, I'm not enjoying it." Instead, I stayed quiet, looked away, and prayed he would get the message.

He didn't really because he then asked if he could make it better with sex, and I laid there thinking, what do I do? What do I say? Will it make it better? I didn't feel mentally or physically ready, and we had already spoken about this earlier, so how do I say it now and not offend him. Instead of saying "No," I said, "I don't know, I'm not sure, I don't know if we should do this." Was he seriously asking me to have sex with him after the conversation we had had earlier that night, or was this a joke? I wasn't quite sure what to make of his question. So I just kept saying, "I don't know," while shaking my head and looking around, trying to figure out how I could get myself out of the situation.

Unfortunately, since I didn't give a direct yes or no answer, he went for it, and maybe a minute or so into it, the pain intensified, and it was excruciating. I shouted, "I can't. It's too much." And when he realized the pain I was in, he backed away, but it was too late. The damage had been done. There was blood on the sheets, and I was extremely embarrassed. I looked up at him and said: "Don't ever speak of this, don't ever tell anyone I was ever here. No one can ever know, you hear me. You don't know who I am. Don't ever tell anyone about this" as tears rolled down my eyes and fear overcame me. Laying on top of me, he looked at me and responded something along the lines of "Don't ever threaten me, I can ruin you in a day, I can have you expelled from your sorority and this school, so you be careful." And with that, I shut up, and he kissed me. Was it supposed to be like this? I don't know, but somehow it felt like I deserved it, I had somehow asked for this. I apologized a million times, feeling like I was stupid for not knowing how to have sex, stupid for thinking I was ready, and disgusting for bleeding on his sheets. I grabbed the covers and asked him where the laundry room was, he took me, and I dropped the sheets in the washer. When we got back upstairs, I looked around the room and knew I needed to go home. He called me an Uber, and I left.

The minute I got in the Uber, tears streamed from my eyes like a waterfall. I was disoriented. When I got to my room, I fell to my knees and sobbed. I couldn't believe I had lost my virginity with someone I didn't care for when I wasn't ready.

I cried violently. I couldn't breathe and began to panic. My neighbor texted me to ask if I was okay. She could hear me crying from her room. It felt like a nightmare. Just like that, I had lost my virginity, something I had fought so hard to keep, something that had meant so much to me. My virginity was more than just something I wanted to keep until marriage, it felt like a part of my identity, my pride. It was mine, and I used to own it, and in one minute, it was gone; all because I didn't have the courage to say no.

I felt weak, powerless, stupid, disgusting, hopeless, broken beyond measure, and ashamed. I didn't want anyone to know, especially not my family or anyone back home. I felt they would have been ashamed and disappointed in me and my poor decisions, especially since my mother had always warned me to stay away from alcohol.

My brain was in overdrive. It berated me:

"Well, you looked for it. No one told you to drink or go to his place after the party!"

"You could have said no, but you didn't."

"Of course you guys had sex. You thought he was going to just have fun with you and NOT have sex LOL."

"How could you have been so stupid?"

"No one will ever want you again, you are damaged goods."

"You're never going to be enough."

"You're not worth it."

"You might as well try to date him so at least it wasn't for nothing."

"If people find out about this, they will never look at you again. Aww, poor Saskia, she was stupid and made a bad decision."

"NO ONE cares, and those that do will be so disappointed and ashamed."

"You might as well shut up and never speak about this."

I had never felt so much self-hate before in my life. I had felt pain, loss, heartache, disappointment, confusion, and depression, but that, no one could have prepared me for. I couldn't make sense of it. I was so good at telling my friends that they are worth the wait, that they get to have the relationships they say they want, and they get to set their standards, yet when it came to myself, I threw it all out the window.

THE MORNING AFTER

The next morning, I woke up hoping it had been a nightmare, something I had dreamed because of how much I had drunk, but as the minutes passed, I knew it was real. I knew I had lost the big V, and there was nothing I could do about it. Every part of me wanted to deny it—it wasn't real, it couldn't be, not me. Not the girl who speaks up and tells people how it is, no way could that be my story. Not the girl who always has it figured out. Yet, there I was. I had lost it, and it was NOTHING like I had imagined. It was a total nightmare, and I couldn't erase it, take it back, change it or get rid of it; it was done. Once again, the reality was too painful to deal with, so I grew numb.

When I went to counseling that week, I knew I had to talk about it but wasn't ready to feel the emotions. I explained to her what happened, and tears began to fill her eyes. I knew then it was real. She felt pain for me because I wasn't ready to feel it for myself. I told her that I wanted to cry but was afraid that if I started, I wouldn't stop like that night. I had lost a huge part of myself, my voice, and my power. I know you may think, "Girl, it was just your virginity, you will survive." I mean, yes, I definitely survived, but to me, at that time, it was more than just my virginity. I had boyfriends break up with me and cheat on me because I wasn't ready to go there, and they were. It was hard for me to let go of those relationships because I cared deeply for them. I had considered sleeping with them so as not to lose them, but I didn't. And I was proud of my determination -- that I chose my values and my self-worth over guys. It was also something that had been instilled in me since childhood, "men want women who are chaste." But then there I was, a few years later, no longer a virgin.

The worst part was that I had no idea how to define or even call that night. My counselor asked if I felt assaulted or raped, and I couldn't even fathom processing her question. I was asking myself what that night meant while also trying to forget about it. I had taken my clothes off, I had chosen to go back to his place, I hadn't said no, but I hadn't said yes. We both had drunk, does that qualify as an assault still, or did it have to be more violent? Did I have to have shouted no for it to count? I couldn't answer the question. I was so angry at myself. How could I have allowed this to happen? I couldn't accept it. I was in a very dark place. I had no emotions, no feelings, I was depressed, I cared for nothing. I drank to forget the shame and guilt. I only wanted to do things that made me feel great, things that brought me pleasure or realistically temporary satisfaction.

I felt invisible and worthless. I thought that everyone could see how broken and disgusting I felt. I became extremely self-conscious, afraid anyone would find out this had happened. Afraid people would see me as the weak, broken girl who couldn't take care of herself. The last thing I wanted to be was the troublesome or burdensome child. I didn't want to feel more unwanted and worse than I already felt, so I pretended like I was perfectly fine. I was living in shame and pain, and no one knew. I kept wondering to myself, will I ever be worth it again? Will God ever forgive me? I told a Catholic friend, and her response was pity and "you need to be careful, you drink too much."

My best friends and family had no idea of the internal turmoil I was in. I wasn't ready for my family and friends to know what happened, especially not after the response I got from that Catholic friend. I was afraid it would ruin my reputation. If the wrong person found out, then everyone would know, and I didn't want that to be my story.

So instead, I kept my mouth shut and suffered in silence alone. I had so many "what-ifs" and "if-you-had-only" scenarios. I was stuck in my world. I told myself that if I was worth anything, I would have never said yes to going home with him, and none of it would have happened. That part of my identity would still be intact, and I would be in control.

I decided to stop feeling and became a woman that didn't care about anything and only wanted to have a good time. In reality, all I wanted was to be loved and comforted, but I was too afraid to ask for support or show vulnerability. So I put on my mask and played a tough, perfect girl act. I didn't need anyone. Or at least that's what I told myself. Lord knows I needed my village more than ever. I just didn't know it then.

I continued with counseling, though. Through her support and help, I was able to start what would be a very long healing journey. It was very slow and painful, but it was a start. I was willing to start. I was willing to start to make different decisions for myself. I couldn't keep living like this. I knew if I stayed on this path of carelessness and continued to pretend I didn't need anybody, my battery would eventually run out.

The first step was awareness: I'm not okay, and I need support.

4

THE BREAKING POINT

Knowing you need support and actually asking or getting that support isn't always so black and white. See, I knew I needed support, but I had no idea what that looked like since I had never asked for it before. Sure, I had experienced counseling which had been a major form of support in my life, but I still had no idea how to ask and receive support in the "real world" from loved ones and family. With my counselor, my mask would come off, and she would get the real authentic Saskia, but with family and friends, I wasn't ready to take off the mask. I was afraid that if I did, they would see me as a burden, as the black sheep of the family or friend group. I was afraid that I had scars and wounds that ran so deep, if they really knew me, they wouldn't want me around. I was convinced I was too broken to be accepted, loved, and worthy. The fear of having them know I'm not "perfect" was immense.

The December after losing my virginity, I had gone home for the holidays as I typically did, except that December, I reached what felt like a point of no return. One night my family and I got into an argument that actually wasn't even centered around me, but I internalized their questions and comments and made it mean that I couldn't do anything right, and I broke. I was so overwhelmed by the shame, guilt, and sadness I had been holding on to, that after that argument—I was beyond empty. I had hit my rock bottom. I was in the darkest place I had ever been. I felt like I was a complete failure who could never make any right decisions and who would never amount to anything. That night, when we got home, all I wanted was a break. I wanted the world to stop for two days so I could take a minute to breathe and recuperate, but I knew that wasn't possible. So I tried to make the world stop. I thought to myself, "If I take five Tylenols, plus considering the amount of alcohol I had drank tonight, that should be enough to put me in a two-day coma maximum since the label says that more than six can cause an overdose. I will take five, plus the alcohol from earlier, and maybe that'll do the coma trick." I was in such a I was in such a dark place that the only way I saw myself continue was through that two-day coma.

I took the pills, and as I was getting into bed, I remember panicking for a couple of seconds, wondering what if I overdid it and ended up in a coma for longer or worse. I was worried that I would become an even bigger burden for my family, so I drank more water and went to sleep praying to God not to kill me but put me in a two-day coma. The next morning when I woke up, I was grateful, but I was also terrified. I was so scared of myself. I couldn't believe how dark I had gotten. I couldn't believe that I had reached a point where I was ready and tried to put myself in a coma to avoid reality. I was so afraid of facing myself and my pain I preferred numbing myself.

That morning, I told myself, "Saskia, you are untrustworthy, and you are dangerous, shut off your feelings, or else you will end up hurting yourself," so I did. I numbed my emotions and feelings and went about my day as if I hadn't just tried to put myself in a coma. The only person I had ever shared this story with before writing it here was my counselor.

I'm sharing it here because I want you to know that I understand what it's like to be in a very dark place. I also know what it's like to be afraid of how dark you can get. I understand that fear and lack of trust that gets created when one tries to hurt themselves. If you've ever been there or discovered a part of yourself you're afraid is too dark to share with others or even admit to yourself, it's okay. Your darkness doesn't make you any less worthy, deserving, or amazing. It's just another part of who you also are. Because without that darkness, the light that shines and radiates from you wouldn't be able to shine so brilliantly. From the darkest places and moments in life come the greatest blessings and breakthroughs. Your darkness is part of your story and self. The more you avoid, the more disconnected you will be to yourself. The more you embrace it and accept it as yours, the more you have control of how it shows up in your life and the more light that can shine through.

I know it may be scary and inconceivable to own certain parts of who you are, especially when they are associated with shame and judgement but remember that we all have our darkness, secrets, and baggage. We all have parts of ourselves that are hard to be with. You're okay. You're not alone, and it's normal. You get to choose the relationship you want to have with it, no one else.

ULTIMATE CHAOS

Junior year of college was the most confusing and awakening year of my life. My counselor had moved on to a different school to continue her degree and get her specialty. I had officially dropped out of my sorority, so I was back to trying to figure out where I fit in, and I was also in the space where I wanted to drop out of college. Since I started, I couldn't wait to graduate, but Junior year was the first year I actually wanted to quit. I knew I couldn't just quit, my options were to at least take a semester or even a year off.

The summer before Junior year started, I turned 20 years old. That year, my birthday wasn't my typical birthday celebration where my friends and family came over to cut a cake and wish me a happy birthday. That year, we couldn't celebrate.

On July 6 and 7th 2018, Haiti went on total lockdown chaos mode. In less than one hour, everyone was stuck where they were, whether it was at home or work. The streets were blocked, there were burning barricades everywhere, people hiding behind walls waiting for you to pass by so they could throw rocks, there was non-stop shooting, and the streets were empty. Never before in my entire life had I seen riots that bad. It felt like Zombieland or an apocalypse movie. If you've ever watched the movie Zombieland or any apocalypse movie, you know how the streets are empty, and there is nothing but burnt cars, trash, and empty buildings. That's how Haiti was, except instead of zombies, we had very angry Haitian men and women who wanted revenge, justice, and explanations. This lockdown began right after Brazil lost in the soccer world cup.

I remember being at the hair salon that afternoon with my mom and my grandmother, who had heard rumors that there were going to be riots, so people should start heading home before the game ended. My grandma, who is afraid of a lot of things, pressured my mom and I to leave and take her home. We were driving in her car that day, so we decided to respect her wishes, and we headed to her house. The plan was to head over and wait for my dad to pick us up on his way home from work. About 2-3 minutes after we got to my grandma's house, guns started firing. We could hear so many gunshots but had no idea where exactly they were coming from. We just knew people were shooting. People in the neighborhood and streets started running, screaming, and the panic began.

A couple of seconds later, we could see fumes and flames from burning tires that were placed further up the road. We called my dad to let him know that we were stuck at my grandma's and to be careful on his way to pick us up. He informed us that the same thing was happening where he was. He was blocked and trying to find a way to get to us. When we called the guy that worked at my house to see if everything was fine up there (we lived in the mountains, about 35 minutes away from my grandma's), he informed us that they had set up barricades (burning tires, tree branches, and rocks) in our neighborhood. At that point, we were in disbelief. To give you some context, where we live is very quiet and whenever there are riots in the city, we never experience them at home, so to hear that there were barricades in front of our neighborhood was a surprise. In the span of two hours, the entire country was on lockdown. To leave your house or wherever you were at that moment was choosing to risk your life and whoever tagged along with you.

My dad was able to get to us in time, but not without having some rocks thrown at his car and running over burning tire barricades. Things finally started to get quieter at 3 AM. At that time, we decided we would take the chance and leave my grandma's house. We wanted to be home. We wanted to check on the house, make sure everything was fine, and we didn't want to be stuck at my grandma's if this lockdown was going to continue for much longer.

The scariest part about this lockdown was that it truly felt like a war zone—it was every man for themselves.

When we left, we saw barricades everywhere, and I mean everywhere. Barricades made from rocks, telephone totem poles, metal scraps, and huge metal garbage disposers were placed in the middle of the road. We kept having to zig zag to find our way home. We connected with a few friends that were also trying to get home and decided to do the drive together. It took us about an hour and a half to get home due to the number of barricades. We also had to turn around once because too many rocks were being thrown at our car, and we had to stop and pay off some people so they could let us pass—it was a nightmare. It sounds crazy and out of a movie, I know, that's exactly how we felt too, but trust me, it was very real.

The next morning, the country was still on lockdown, everything was closed, and no one was leaving their homes. I remember my dad's phone ringing non-stop. The phones at our house never stopped buzzing. We were constantly being updated on possible riots and lootings in the area. There were rumors that people were going to come to our house and burn it down, and that was pretty intense and scary.

That day, I truly felt ready to go to war. I remember telling my dad that I was ready to fight and fire a gun if we needed to. I had gone shooting with him and my brother a couple of times prior, and I remember thinking to myself, today, we may have to kill people because this situation may become a matter of life or death. It sounds very dramatic and intense, but that's how I viewed the situation. It became even more real when a crowd of 10-15 people started to argue in front of our gate, and my dad had to talk to them to calm them down. My dad was talking to them for about an hour or two.

My dad came back upstairs, and I remember telling him I was ready if he needed back up. He laughed and told me that it wasn't necessary, but if he needed it, he already had a plan, and he would let me know. After a while, the crowd got smaller and smaller, and eventually, they all went home. That night, I was worried that someone would break into our homes and murder us in our sleep. After a couple of days, things started to open up again, and people started to circulate again in the streets as if nothing had happened, as if Haiti hadn't been a complete and total no-man zone. As if no one else had lived that lockdown.

BUT, I THOUGHT IT WOULD ALWAYS BE HOME

My birthday, which occurred a few days later, was not very eventful. Because of all that had just occurred, we didn't feel it was the right time to celebrate. Instead, we cut a cake as a family and stayed home. A couple of days later, my mom and I left Haiti and went to Miami to get me settled in for my Junior year.

I remember going into Junior year thinking it was a chance to start new. I no longer had to attend sorority events or make up reasons as to why I couldn't attend meetings. I had one less obligation, and it felt amazing. I was excited to turn a new leaf.

I started to plan a solo self-discovery trip to Asia. I planned to go there over the summer and find myself. I wasn't too sure how to go about it, so I asked people I knew who had traveled solo before and got advice and tips from them. One of my best friend's loved the idea of traveling to Asia for seven weeks, so he told me he would join me. I was so excited. It felt like it could actually happen because it wasn't just me planning it anymore —I had someone else tagging along. My brother was getting married in March of the next year, so we decided that we would confirm everything and book our flights around that time since it was a summer trip. In the meantime, I decided to reconnect with my faith and attend church more often. I would go to adoration and talk to my priest more often. I remember being so excited about this trip and telling him about how great it would be, and his response was that I didn't have to go all the way to Asia to find myself—I could find it right where I was. At the time, that was a concept I was not open to hearing because I was set on Asia. I had engraved in my mind that my self-discovery was going to happen there. As time passed, my best friend and I stopped planning and talking about it as much, but it was still in the back of my mind.

A couple of months later, my mom flew to Miami because there were supposed to be riots similar to the ones that happened in July, and she couldn't handle the same stress and pressure we had experienced then. I was so happy to have my mom with me for those couple of days. I had no idea that that trip would change everything for us. When she came back from that trip, my brother told her that they had to leave Haiti because the stress and insecurity was overbearing. It wasn't safe for them to live in Haiti anymore.

A couple of days after my mom got back to Haiti, she had to pack a suitcase and leave. She called me on the phone to tell me that she was leaving and had no idea where she was going to go or what they were going to do, but she knew it was time to leave. My parents didn't have time to pack their belongings, say goodbye or tell people they were leaving— they just left. I was worried, but in my mind, it was temporary, so it would be over soon, and before I knew it, they would be back home. Little did I know.

A couple of days later, my aunt called me to ask me what I wanted from my room because she and other family members were packing it up. I understood what she was telling me, but I couldn't quite seem to process it. I remember telling her to take my clothes because it was all I could remember leaving. I couldn't even process what was happening, so there was no way I could think about what I had or had not left behind. I just knew I had left clothes behind because they weren't currently in my closet, but everything else was a blur. I wasn't ready to accept that my room being packed up meant that we were moving out. I did what I knew best to cope—I detached myself from the situation and went numb.

Later that week, my parents called me to tell me that they were going to put the house up for rent, and I knew that meant that the home I had grown up in and lived in for the past 20 years was gone. I was heartbroken and in disbelief. A part of me wanted to hope that by the new year, we would be back home.

ISOLATED AND ALONE

Through all my ups and downs, I could always talk to people if I chose to, but most of the time, I chose not to because I either didn't feel ready or I was afraid of judgments. This time though, even if I wanted to talk to someone, I couldn't. No one was safe to talk to. I had my parents, but I felt like they had too much to handle at the time, so I didn't want to be a burden or something more for them to worry about. My grandparents were handling enough on their own, and I didn't think my brother would understand—so I kept to myself. I felt they all already had enough on their plate. I couldn't tell friends because it wasn't safe for my family, and I couldn't tell my coworkers because God forbid it got out to the wrong person. I felt trapped. Never before had I felt so secluded and alone.

Since I couldn't tell my friends and loved ones what was really happening in my life and with my family, I chose to distance myself and disconnect. I even deleted Instagram for a year. I was holding on to so many secrets, and I no longer had it in me to want to connect. Connecting with others meant performing, lying, and pretending to be doing great and I was too exhausted mentally, emotionally, and physically to keep doing that. I completely disconnected. My thought process was, "if people can't reach me, they can't ask how I'm doing."

It was a very challenging time because I was suffering a lot; trying to understand what my life was supposed to look like and what I was supposed to do. I began to question everything again. Who was I? What was my purpose? What was home? What was going to happen to us? Would we ever be a normal family again? Would we ever go back home? Did that mean I didn't have to move back to Haiti? What was I supposed to do with my Public Health degree? I began to question it all. I was starting to realize that my life as I know it had completely changed, and I had no idea what was next. Home was no longer home.

I was so overwhelmed by everything that I wanted to take a break from life once again. I wanted to stop and take a breath. I wanted a semester or year off so I could figure it out. I started to look into being an inactive student and what the process looked like. I found out that I could take a semester or year off and come back to school and not lose any credits or anything. When I got back, I would continue where I left off. I decided that I was going to take a semester off to figure out what I really wanted to do. I called my brother and told him that I needed his help to tell mom and dad that I was going to take a semester off. He asked me what I would do in the meantime, and I told him about this program in Asia where young people went to discover themselves. It was an intense outdoor program, but I was ready for it. I needed a life change. He told me to sleep on it and get my plan ready because he would help me pitch the idea to my parents. I finally started to see the light—I was hopeful that the breath I had been waiting for was finally coming.

I went to sleep that night, excited at the idea that I wouldn't come back to campus after my December break. I would be traveling to Asia to discover myself. The trip I wanted was happening faster than I had imagined. The next day though, my brother called me. He told me that he had slept on it, and after giving it a lot of thought, he didn't think it was the time for me to do it. He asked me how many semesters I had left, and I told him three. He then told me to brave through them. He said he understood how I felt but that our parents had sacrificed so much for me to go to the University of Miami and get this education that it wouldn't make sense to leave now. The light I had seen was beginning to dim. I knew what he was saying, and I knew he was right because I knew that the minute I went to Asia, I would never go back to school. I knew the importance of education and how privileged I was to get this opportunity, so I decided to brave through it.

I began to look into other majors and even transferring to different universities, but everything I thought of switching to meant that I would graduate a year later, and I was *so* ready to graduate, so that wasn't an option. I stopped trying to find a way out and surrendered to what was in front of me. I decided to look at the bright side of life: my parents were healthy and safe, I was at a great University getting a degree that would help many people, and I had only three semesters left. I was right by the finish line, almost there.

During Thanksgiving, I flew to Orlando to be with friends and family. I always loved going to Orlando. It was an amazing escape, and the community there made me feel at home. I used to go to Orlando almost every month because of how much I loved it there. When I was looking at other schools to transfer to, the University of Central Florida was the first one I looked at. I knew that if I moved there, I would have a little community that would love and support me, but I also didn't want to be in school for an additional year, so I didn't go through with the transfer. When I went to Orlando that Thanksgiving, no one had any idea what I was going through, I was always the life of the party, the energetic one that never stops being happy. In Orlando, I wasn't faking it. I was genuinely happy because I was surrounded by people who didn't remind me of the stuff I was dealing with back home. When I was there, all that mattered was what was happening in Orlando. It was like we were in our own bubble, and I loved it. It was the best escape from reality.

However, one evening, while I was in Orlando texting my best friend that I was planning on traveling with, I got very overwhelmed. He was asking me questions about the holidays as we were both planning on spending it in Haiti and his questions brought up everything I had tried so hard to bottle up and hide.

He was the person I trusted the most in my life, the one person I felt like like I could purge my heart to and not a soul would find out. He knew my secrets and my past and never once judged me or pitied me for any of it. I trusted my secrets were safe with him, and as I couldn't hold on anymore, I called him and told him what my family was going through. He was very surprised and had a hard time processing it himself. I didn't give him details, but I told him that home was no longer home and that my family would most likely never live there again. I told him how scary and heartbreaking it was for me because I didn't want to fly to Haiti in December. I wasn't ready to face the music that was my life. He didn't say much, but he empathized, and at that moment, that's all I needed. He even ended our call by hyping me up, telling me we would have a great December nonetheless. That was my first experience of sharing vulnerably, being seen, and being heard.

When I went "home" that December, I stayed with my brother and sister-in-law. I partied every day and avoided reality. I was a MESS though, I got drunk every single time I went out, and not just the "I can't walk drunk" but the "let me share my heart out and feelings to the entire world type of drunk." It was ugly, it was messy, and the following mornings I would wake up ashamed and disgusted with myself. One night, I was so drunk and done with the entire night, as we were entering the parking lot of my brother's building, I opened the door and rolled out of the moving car. I remember my friends stopping the car and being like, WTF SASKIA?! I ran up the stairs until I got to the last floor and sat on the floor sobbing. It had been too much, and I couldn't hold it all in anymore, especially not with the amount of alcohol I had. I am grateful for my best friends that were there with me that night as they followed me up the stairs and took care of me. They were very confused and upset, but they showed up for me nonetheless, comforted me, and reassured me that I wasn't crazy for feeling the way I felt. They reminded me of who I was.

TURNING PAGES

When 2019 began, I was so sad—I was at my breaking point. I was surrounded by the people I loved the most, yet I felt so lonely. The pain, wounds, and baggage I was carrying were weighing me down like never before. I wasn't excited about the new year because the last three years had been horrible for me. I could only imagine what that new year was going to bring. I braced myself for more turmoil, pain, and heartache, but 2019 surprised me.

Earlier, I spoke about going on a trip to Asia. As the new year had rolled in, my best friend and I started to plan it more. We reached out to different people and places we wanted to go and experiences we wanted to have; we were getting everything ready so that we could finalize it in the next couple of months. Some complications began to arise with our trip and plan, and we started to question it a lot. Some of the places we wanted to visit we were warned against, and my parents became weary—they weren't as comfortable with our trip anymore. My parents also hoped that Asia was a phase I would get over since it hadn't been the first time I had mentioned I wanted to travel there. Then, I started dating someone and had to reconsider the entire trip. My partner then was actually very supportive of this trip. He was pro-trip and wanted me to go but also had some reservations as I would be going with another guy friend who was single and heterosexual. I began to question this trip myself, wondering what could happen during that trip. We would be spending a lot of time together, discovering new cultures, new land, new countries, and we would be traveling for seven weeks. There was a lot to think about.

The more I thought about it, and the more I spoke to my partner and family about it, I felt like going on that trip wasn't the right decision for the time. I didn't trust myself. I didn't trust that nothing was going to happen, so I canceled the trip. It felt like the right choice to make even though I didn't want to make it, and I felt terrible about it. I knew I would be disappointing someone who'd stood by my side every single time I needed it, and that killed me. I was scared of the trip and scared of falling for him and having him not feel the same way. I was scared of my partner breaking up with me because of the long distance. I was scared that I would cheat on my partner. Asia was filled with uncertainties, and I wasn't ready for more disappointments in my life. So I chose the safe option—I cancelled Asia and instead planned a solo trip to Hawai'i.

5

RUDE AWAKENING

*H*awai'i was the beginning of my awakening. It was the first time in my life that I got to experience such a different culture and life than what I'd ever known or seen on television. I had heard of living a simple and stress-free life, but I didn't think it really existed. I had traveled to many countries before, like the Dominican Republic, Greece, France, Spain, Italy, Monaco, Croatia, Mexico, and the Bahamas but never before had I experienced what I experienced in Hawai'i. When I canceled my trip to Asia, I was still determined to go on a self-discovery trip, so instead, I chose to go to Hawai'i. My sister-in-law had suggested it as one of my aunts lived there, and I agreed it was a great alternative.

My trip to Hawai'i is one that shifted my core in so many ways. I got to meet and connect with some of the most genuine and open people. Auntie Paula, Zeke, Lee, and my aunt made my trip one I will cherish forever. They introduced me to a new way of living. They treated me like family, and I felt like I had known them my entire life. Even though I was a thousand miles away from family and what I considered home, this new place felt homey and welcoming.

We were on the Big Island and stayed mostly on the Hilo side. I got to travel around the entire island and visit caves, waterfalls, volcanoes, black sand beaches, green sand beaches, and so much more. One of my favorite places on the island was Pahoa. Pahoa is considered the "hippie" side of the island. It's the side where everyone and every lifestyle is welcomed and accepted. It's a place where authenticity is not only embraced, but it's encouraged. It's a place where most people invite you to be yourself fully and to embrace all that you bring to this earth and life. It was such a different approach and experience from anything I'd encountered. Growing up, we were raised and educated to follow certain rules, standards, mannerisms, and appearances, and there I was in a place that said, "screw it" to all of that and said, "Just be You—whatever that looks like to you." It was very weird for me. I thought these people were on some high drugs because the level of acceptance and freedom felt extremely uncomfortable. It turns out they were just people who had experienced enough of the world telling them who they needed to be and instead decided to choose for themselves who they wanted to be.

While I couldn't quite understand that lifestyle and mindset yet, I loved observing it and getting to witness it. I loved that no one cared who I was, what I wore, or even what I did. Everyone minded their own business and wished me the best of luck with mine. I loved that I could wear leggings and a t-shirt to go to dinner, and that was perfectly acceptable. I didn't have to go above and beyond and wear make-up and heels—no—I just had to show up, and that was enough.

When I first got to Hawai'i, and we would go out for the day or for dinner, I would get very cute and dressed up, and when we would get to our destination, I would feel overdressed. It took me a couple of days to stop doing my automatic— putting on a "perfect" face/look for everyone. I slowly began to let go and to just be myself. I wore my leggings that I love and enjoy wearing so much. I wore tennis shoes and t-shirts and didn't take 20 minutes to do my hair. I would wash it, brush it, and just start my day. I didn't overthink my look, I knew I felt great, and that's all that mattered in the moment. Growing up in a society where the way you dress, the places you go, and the things you do define who you are or the way people choose to view and judge you, it was liberating not to have to think about that or care for that matter. I also got to be adventurous and try new things like learning how to play with silks and hoops. I learned how to garden and drive, and most importantly, I learned to start to let go and just be myself.

Sundays in Hawai'i were my favorite. I would go to Mass (Catholic Sunday Church Service) in the morning, and afterward, my aunt and I would go to ecstatic dance. When I first heard "Ecstatic dance", coming from Haiti, I thought it was some spiritual folkloric type of dance and was very on edge. But since I love to dance and I was in Hawai'i to discover myself and try new adventures, I decided to go and try it out. When I got there, I was unsure of what to expect at first, but then I fell in love with it.

Ecstatic dance is a style of dance where all is allowed. There is no right or wrong way to dance. It was the first time I attended a dance class that felt so sacred, freeing, and empowering. Before I could even enter the dancefloor, I had to take off my shoes, leave my phone and read the rules. The rules stated that I agreed to stay silent, not touch anyone, and respect everyone's space. Everyone there respected the rules. Each person that was on the dancefloor seemed like they were in their own bubble, their own world. They didn't care who was watching or what was happening. They were just dancing and moving. They were feeling the rhythm of the music and the drums, and they were just dancing to it. It was pretty interesting to watch at first because, again, I had never experienced people dancing just to dance. They were dancing because they felt it in their bones and at their core. I could tell that these people weren't there to perform but to be, feel, and let go.

I wanted to dance like they were dancing, not a care in the world, but what was happening right here and there. I was so stuck in my head for the first 30 minutes that I couldn't dance. I was swaying side to side, but I was rigid. I was in full performance mode, trying to find the right thing to do, of course. After 30 or so minutes, I realized I was never going to figure it out because there had never been a right way to do it. The only "right" way to do it was to let go and just move. I decided to let go by closing my eyes and moving my body. At first, it felt more like I was stretching, but the more I tuned in, the more I got lost in the music and the rhythm, the more I began to let go. The more I let go, the more I moved, the more I danced. If my arm felt like going up, I allowed it to go up. If I felt like jumping, I began to jump. If I felt like twirling, I twirled. After 10 or so minutes of surrendering and listening to my body, I was in a different space. I was in "Nirvana". I was dancing to dance, and I was having a blast. I remember dancing with this old lady that was probably in her late 60s or early 70s, and all we did was look at each other, smile, and move. By the end of the ecstatic dance, we were hugging one another as if we had known each other. We had created a connection through dance, and never once had we spoken to each other, but we understood one another through our movements and body language. We were both there to experience surrender, joy, and freedom, and so we did. Even as I think about her right now, I am filled with joy and gratitude because I still remember the connection and acceptance we created through dance. I left that morning feeling sourced and wishing they hosted ecstatic dance every morning.

After dancing on Sundays, we would go to the beach. It was a naked beach where most of the Ecstatic dance crew would go. When I first got there, I was amazed. 1) I had never been to a naked beach before 2) to get to this beach we had to hike down this little mountain/cliff as it wasn't a typical, popular, or known beach—it was a beach that only a select few knew about. When we got to the bottom of the cliff/mountain, the sand was black. The black sand is due to the eroded lava fragments and volcanic minerals, and it was beautiful. Just miles of black sand layed out with the ocean waves crashing in and out. The waves were taller than any waves I'd seen before, and I could tell there was such a strong current in the water. It was blissful.

It was atypical for me to see senior citizens and toddlers walking around naked on the same beach, and oddly enough, at the same time, it felt comforting—reassuring me that this was a safe space to just be. I mean, how much safer can it get? 30 or so people walking, eating, talking, swimming, dancing around naked. I couldn't help but wonder how they felt so comfortable. I wasn't even naked, and I was so self-conscious. The first couple of Sundays, I didn't even want to put on my bathing suit because I didn't think I looked good enough, so I couldn't even imagine walking around naked, especially in broad daylight.

At the beach, they also had drum circles. They created an atmosphere of fun, joy, and sacredness. My aunt would dance all day and twirl to the sound of the drums, and I would watch her get immersed in her environment, and it made me happy. I loved experiencing her world and getting to meet her people and know her in a different way. We didn't grow up together, her living in Hawai'i and me living in Haiti. We had maybe seen each other 4 or 5 times in our lives before I made that trip, so it was awesome to experience her world.

Some Sundays, I would meet people I had seen at the Ecstatic dance earlier, and some others, I would meet people I had never met before. I always enjoyed the conversations I had there because I was constantly meeting new people and exposing myself to a whole new way of living and being. Hawai'i was a world of possibility to me— anything and everything felt possible and safe to try. I was amazed by what looked like stress-free living. These people had families, bills, and responsibilities, yet they somehow made it look like they had no worries or stress. Everyone was friendly, welcoming, loving, and it felt like one big family. I later learned that it wasn't so much stress-free living as much as it was authentic living.

In the evenings, when the sun was about to set, we would hike back up to the top and go to the lawn. The lawn was this great big field of grass, literally right up the cliff from the beach. It looked like a huge family picnic. Most of the people from the beach would come up, and when we would get there, there would already be so many other people eating, dancing, picnicking, playing with fire, ropes, selling vegan baked goods, and there was an even bigger drum circle.

On the lawn, we danced, played, and became kids again. I loved Sunday Fundays. Each week, I would learn more and more about the art of letting go of pretending and performing. I would slowly stop caring about whether or not people were looking at me, assessing me, or judging me.

I began to dance in the drum circles and wear my bathing suit to the beach. I would interact with the locals and attend other events with them. I was slowly becoming more comfortable with my body and myself. I was leaning into authenticity and freedom.

When we didn't have our typical Sunday Funday, Zeke or Auntie Paula and Gayle would take me out on adventures. We would visit farmer's markets, hike up volcanoes, waterfalls, caves, and visit/tour Kona which was on the other side of the island. We never had any concrete plans, but every day I knew an adventure awaited us.

It was the first time that I got to see adults living life without a set schedule. They didn't work a 9-5. They created their own schedules based on what they needed. I felt like they were always on vacation, but really they weren't. They were working hard and doing it in their own way. They were choosing how they were working and making a living for themselves. I began to realize that life didn't have to be as black and white as I grew up thinking it was.

My future and life didn't have to look the same as my parents or loved ones. I could choose the life I wanted to live. I could live an authentic, safe and free life by the beach where I got to create my own schedule. I could attend Ecstatic dance and travel when I wanted to. I could meet people from very different backgrounds and experiences and still create deep, meaningful connections. I could live a completely different life than I'd ever known possible.

I left Hawai'i awed. I went home knowing there was a whole other world out there filled with possibilities I had yet to experience.

Mahalo Tūtū Pele.

6

THE ROAD LESS TRAVELED

"Am I really going to do this?"

"Am I really ready for this?"

"Oh gosh, it's about to happen!"

J couldn't believe I was finally about to do it.

For about four years, I had told myself I wanted to shave my head, but I was terrified. I asked my family what they thought about me shaving my head, and they thought it was a terrible idea. They knew how much I cared about the way I looked, and especially the way my hair looked, so they were worried that if I did go through with it, I would be extremely unhappy. They would remind me that if I shaved it, I wouldn't be able to change it. I would have to live with that. And so, every time I would muster up the courage, I would back down soon after, afraid I would become uglier, and people would like me even less.

I was so attached to looking good and having the "perfect" hair that I was miserable in my own skin. Growing up in Haiti, I was always told that having straight hair was the pretty and acceptable thing to do and have. Since the age of 8 years old, I have had relaxers and texturizers to keep my hair straight. I was obsessed with my hair. If my hair didn't look good, I was having the worst day. If people loved my hair, it was the best day. A major part of my identity and how I saw myself relied on my hair.

I had allocated so much of my worth to my hair; how long or how straight it was, how I could or couldn't style, how "natural" or flowy it looked. It was always about how it looked so that other people would see it as acceptable, desirable, or "proper". It's ironic to think of now because it was so far from being natural or "flowy". It was constant work and manipulation to make it look the way it was "supposed to look".

I even had extensions in my freshman year of college because 1) I was balding and wanted to cover it up, and 2) I thought people would actually like me better if I had longer and straighter hair. I would spend a fortune on tape-in extensions and hair salons because I wanted to look perfect. I would buy the best real human hair and the best invisible extensions just to have it seem natural, when truthfully, it was the complete opposite. It was all so superficial, but in my mind, as long as people couldn't tell it wasn't the real deal, then it could pass as real, similar to "fake it till you make it."

I was embarrassed to say I had relaxers and texturizers growing up because people made fun of me for it. I had someone once compare my hair to the hair of their housekeeper, and the reason that hurt was not because she was a housekeeper, but because I knew that it was said to hurt me, to make me feel less than, and it worked—I was hurt, and I felt less than. When I was old enough to choose what I wanted to put in my hair, I switched to the Brazilian Keratin straightening treatment because it was more "acceptable" as it was the treatment women with straighter hair would put in their own hair. Somehow, that made me feel like I was closer to having "good" hair, even though it was doing the same thing the relaxers and texturizers were. It was mental.

In my mind, as long as it was the Keratin treatment, it was better and accepted. I was one step closer to fitting the mold that Haitian men and women considered beautiful, desirable, and/or enough. I was trying so hard to fit in perfectly into that mold. I wanted to be accepted and seen as beautiful and desirable, so I did whatever it took. The worst part is that even though I was doing all these things to look "perfect", I was miserable on the inside. On the outside, I would look good and check all the boxes, but on the inside, I was pretty shallow. It was all a beautiful facade that I was so used to portraying. I actually believed it to be my truth.

MY CHOICE

My Senior year of college, my cousin invited me to attend a transformational training she had completed. I was very hesitant to attend at first, not sure what to expect from it. It sounded interesting but I wasn't enrolled. After a couple back and forths and my trip to Hawai'i, I accepted her invitation and she signed me up for the August training. It was a three-part training. The first part was called Discovery. It exposed me to my automatic way of operating in life. It showed me my patterns, the way I self-sabotaged and how I lived in survival mode 90% of the time versus actually living. I was learning so much about myself that I knew I wanted and needed to complete the rest of the training. It was my first experience of having a coach and I was loving every second of it.

During my part two of the transformational training, I was paired up with a buddy. When I first saw her, I instantly disliked her. She had a beautiful smile and was so welcoming, yet for some reason, there was something about her that frustrated me. As the training went on and we got to know each other, I began to realize why I disliked her so much. She had something I wanted but didn't dare to have. She had the natural, curly short hair I wasn't bold enough to have. She was comfortable in her skin, and I envied her for it. When I saw her, I thought: "Man, I wonder what that would feel like. What would it look like if I cut my hair and started to do stuff for myself?" I thought about it, and later that evening, I shared it with her. She told me how liberating and empowering it was for her and encouraged me to do it myself if I wanted it so badly, but I wasn't ready —not yet, at least.

Thursday night, before the training day ended, I made the decision to shave my head the next morning. I asked her to come along with me because I was terrified and she had done it, so if anyone could understand, it was her. She was so excited and couldn't wait to tag along the next morning. I was also excited, but I was petrified. What would people say? How will my family react? Will I hate it? How will I look? I had so many questions, so many fears, and so much uncertainty, but I knew it was time.

That night, for the first time, I sent my mom a voice message letting her know I was going to shave my head. I didn't ask her for permission, validation, or approval. This time I asked her for support. I told her that what I needed from her was to remind me that I was beautiful on days I would feel ugly or forget. I also told her that I didn't want her opinion on whether or not I should do it because I was going to do it, and all I needed was her emotional support. I was anxious about her reply, afraid she would be angry or disappointed with my decision. Instead, she utterly surprised me.

She called me the next morning as I was on my way to cut my hair and told me I had her full support. She definitely had a lot of questions, but she wasn't questioning my decisions, just making sure I knew what I was getting myself into. She reminded me that she would always support me, even if she didn't understand or see eye to eye, that she would always be there, right by my side. My mom showed up for me that day in a way I hadn't known was possible, and it was all because I allowed her to surprise me. I gave her the chance to show up and be the supportive mom in my life. In the past, I would have kept her in the dark, but that day, something changed—I got to experience vulnerability, leaning in for support, and receiving it. Thank you, mams, for showing up for me and having me experience something different in our relationship. I see you, I love you, and I honor you.

SEPTEMBER 6TH, 2019

It's funny how my ego works. The next morning I overslept my alarm and did not show up to my scheduled hair appointment at the salon with my buddy and our friend who was also doing the training with us. I woke up when she called me to ask where I was because they were at the hair salon, but it was closed. When I realized I had overslept, I was so embarrassed, I told her what had happened, and she asked me if I was serious about cutting my hair. She said if I wasn't ready, we didn't have to go through with it, but I needed to decide at that moment because time was passing by, and the third day of training was going to begin soon.

I thought about it for a second and assured her I was ready. I didn't know where else I could go to cut my hair, but she had already thought of a backup plan. She laughed and asked me how committed I was to doing it—I told her it was now or never. She said: "Okay, we're going to Supercuts!" If I was freaking out before about cutting my hair, this took it to a whole other level. Not only was I about to shave my head, but I was about to do it at a Supercuts, like WHAT!

I started thinking of all the ways this could go very south, but in the end, I was committed and ready for this transformation. I knew that the time was now.

They came to pick me up, and before we headed to Supercuts, we picked up another friend along the way to join us for the adventure. He had no idea what was happening until we started driving towards Supercuts. He was so excited and surprised. He couldn't wait for us to get there. I, on the other hand, was terrified. Never before had I done something so bold and outrageous. I was the type of girl that would text five to six different people before posting a picture on Instagram, and here I was on my way to Supercuts to shave my head, and I wasn't asking for anyone's permission (the small wins).

When we got there, the hairdresser was a Dominican woman. I will never forget her expression when I told her that I was there to shave my head. She was so confused and shocked. She couldn't understand why I wanted to shave my head. She kept telling me my hair was healthy and long. She did not want me to cut it. After some back and forth and convincing, she finally agreed. How funny that I had to enroll her into cutting my hair when I was terrified of doing it. I could have easily walked out and said, "Whelp, she did not want to do it," but I kept going back because it was time.

It had been so long since I had had my hair natural I had no idea what it looked like. I asked her to cut my hair until the part where my natural hair was growing in, but I had recently done a keratin treatment, so I barely had any new growth. She kept telling me that I would have no hair because I had no growth, and I kept telling her that I understood and knew what I was asking for. After another couple of minutes of back and forth, she sat me down, and it began. My buddy was filming and taking pictures of the entire process.

When the shaving began, I think I stopped breathing for a while. I was in shock and paralysis mode. I was actually doing it, and there was no turning back. The hair was falling, and it was becoming lighter and lighter. My buddy was filming, our friends were smiling, and one of them even kept saying, "Oh shit," "that's so dope," "damn, Saskia, you're really doing it." All I could do was stare at myself and try to process what was actually happening. I was taking it in while also being paralyzed that it was actually happening. There was no turning back now.

After she finished cutting it, I had a one-level haircut (imagine a man with extremely short hair). I wasn't bald, but I had no hair, I couldn't brush it, and nothing could mess it up because there was nothing to brush or mess up. I stared at myself, wondering, "who the heck is this person?" I couldn't recognize myself.

I was raw, bare, naked, and I was no longer invisible. It was like having no hair had me stand out more because I could literally notice people looking at me and turning around just to see me walk down the street. It was weird for me to be seen in that way; I felt naked and vulnerable. I no longer had my hair as my mask or shield to hide behind. There was no more cover. It was me, myself, and I. I was raw, and I was real. It was the most authentic I had ever been in my twenty-one years.

I will never forget people's reactions when I showed up to the training Friday morning with no hair. Believe it or not, there were people on our team that hadn't noticed me before then. Some people thought my hair was always shaved and those that had seen me were in disbelief. They couldn't recognize me.

Those who hadn't noticed me before then made me realize that people didn't see me when I was faking it and pretending to be "perfect" and having it all together. I was almost invisible. But when I showed up raw, bare, naked, and vulnerable, they saw me. They saw the real me, and they actually noticed me for the first time. I went from being invisible and unnoticed to "Woah, Saskia's in the room," and that felt pretty incredible.

September 6th, 2019, was the day I began my self-love journey. It's the day I decided to start living for myself. The day I began to breathe and catch my breath again. The day I chose Saskia. That day, I didn't just cut my hair. On September 6th, 2019, I woke up. I let go of my attachment to my hair and to what society thinks is the right thing or the right way to look. That day I stepped into a gigantic pool of unknown and uncertainty. I took the biggest leap I'd ever taken in my life, and it was the best decision I've ever made —the decision to love me, bare and raw.

I learned to love myself from ground zero, to look at myself every day in the mirror, and say I love you. To touch my hair and scalp every day and say thank you for keeping me warm, for making me be unique, for growing, for being patient with me as I treated you like crap. Thank you hair for teaching me so much about myself. Now that I didn't have my hair to hide behind or to use as my determinant of my value, I had to look inward and find out who I really was when everything I put so much value and importance on got stripped away. It was the time for me to be with me in a way I had never gotten the chance or taken the time to do so.

7

LIGHTHOUSE

On the Friday morning of my part two training, I got up in front of my entire team, a group of about 40 or some people, and exposed my biggest insecurity and fear; how I look and feel about myself. I was vulnerable, I was real, I was messy. I told them how unlovable and ugly I felt, and I even cried in front of them. During the day, we were put into small groups, and we had the opportunity to share our most painful memories. For me, it was losing the big V. I was petrified of sharing that story. Sharing that story meant I would have to be honest and extremely vulnerable. It would require me to open a door I sealed long ago. My most painful memory was the night I lost my virginity. As my teammates began to share, tears began to fill my eyes as I empathized with their stories and as the fear of being seen as less than increased. I went last, hoping we would have run out of time and I wouldn't have needed to go. My small group looked at me as my lips quivered and my hands shook. I couldn't even look at them. I was looking down, they were holding my hand, and after a couple of seconds, I looked up and saw two of my teammates looking at me with so much compassion and empathy, I started tearing up. Their eyes said: "It's okay, we've got you. You can share." One of them squeezed my hand as the tears streamed down my face, and with every squeeze and head nod, I felt stronger to share and to allow the pain to take over. I started to feel it was safe for me to share.

The minute I started to tell my story, I began to sob, I couldn't talk or even finish the story, but they understood. They knew the story I was telling. The pain, the shame, the guilt was overwhelming me. It was like I was reliving the moment all over again. It was very hard and painful to say out loud that I felt taken advantage of, stupid, worthless, and powerless. Stupid for putting so much value on my virginity and stupid for having gone there that night, worthless for being treated like I was nothing, and powerless because I did nothing to stop it. It was hard to admit what happened to me, let alone a group of people I had met three days ago.

I cried so much that day. There was snot everywhere, my eyes were puffy, I was sweating, I was gagging, and I was a whole mess. In my mess, they showed up for me. They loved on me, hugged me, saw me, heard me, and even acknowledged me. They made me feel like my experience, and my pain was not a burden.

My healing process was continuing, and while it felt painful, it also alleviated some of the weight and heaviness I felt. I was transforming and shifting so many parts of myself. It was the most real and authentic I'd felt since that trip to Hawai'i. For the first time, I was allowing people to finally see the deepest parts of me, not just the parts I thought they wanted to see. They were seeing the real me, the me that wants to be loved and seen, the me that's terrified that no one will ever love me enough to stick around, the me that feels like all men see when they see me is a vagine, the me that thought I was ugly, and the me that was willing to get messy to breakthrough my traumas, past and stories.

While it was the scariest thing I had ever tried, it was also the most liberating thing. I was getting a taste of what it felt like to be Saskia—authentically and fully. I wasn't just the smiling, happy Saskia, I was also the wounded, scared Saskia. I learned that when I truly allow people to see me and allow them to show up, support, and love me, they surprise me and exceed my expectations. My team saw me, heard me, loved me, and cheered me on when I showed up authentic and raw. They didn't care that I had no hair, felt broken and dealt with a lot of trauma. They acknowledged me for it. They didn't care to connect with the "perfect" Saskia because that Saskia is shallow, superficial, and lives in constant denial and performance. The Saskia they were getting to know was afraid, authentic, vulnerable, and real. I was practicing something completely foreign to me: vulnerability.

Brené Brown, I was daring greatly, I was in the arena! I practiced it, I was there, and I am still practicing every day. The more I shared my insecurities and fears, the less power they had over me. The messier I got, the more support I received, and the more I shared, the more I healed. The first step of my self-love journey had begun: vulnerability.

ONE STEP ONE DAY AT A TIME

As I went through my transformational process, it was very challenging for me to learn how to open up to those who hadn't been in the training because we hadn't established a relationship where I knew or felt it was safe for me to be vulnerable and messy. I had no idea how to reconnect with the "real" world. I was trying to balance my old lifestyle while also trying to apply what I had experienced in the training with my team, but it was challenging. I had put a mask on for so long, and I didn't know what it looked like to have it off in the "real world". It was easy to do it in the training room because the trainers and coaches had created a safe environment for us to be vulnerable, authentic, and messy. There was no room for judgment in the training room, it was acceptance and love, but out in the real world, I had no idea how people would respond. My experience of the "real world" was judgement and rejection. I was terrified of the judgments and feedback I was going to get. Who was I supposed to be now? How was I supposed to continue living this new transformation and truth in a world that still felt unsafe and scary to me? I didn't know the answer, but I assumed it would be a lot of trial and error and continuing to practice asking and receiving support from my family, loved ones, and people despite the fears and stories I had made up about asking and receiving support.

What I expected to happen after my transformational training was that it would have fixed all of my problems. I would have come back having it all figured out—healed and perfect. What I actually learned was that transformation and growth are a journey. It's a process, and it's not linear. Even after all the learning, experiencing and doing the work for six months, I still fell back into old patterns. I still made similar mistakes, and I still continued to self-sabotage. I have had to learn that becoming aware doesn't mean I won't make mistakes again. It just means that now I will have a better awareness which can allow me to start to choose differently. Creating new declarations and setting new boundaries doesn't mean I won't fall back into old habits and patterns. Those setbacks only confirm that I am human—I am ever growing and learning. Transformation, self-discovery, and healing are trial and error processes. It's never-ending, and while that may sound terrifying, there is an odd sense of comfort and ease knowing that there is no time frame, there is no right or wrong way to go about it—there is just the way and time frame you choose. There are always new possibilities available.

Since I started my journey, I have had countless setbacks and breakdowns, I have fallen back into old patterns of seeking validation from men to define my worth, I have lost friends, I have been rejected, I have failed, I have lied, and I have cried so many times. And while my journey has been one with many bumps and obstacles, I have also learned to say no, I have learned to set boundaries in my relationships, and I have learned to ask and receive support from my colleagues, family, friends, and even strangers. Most importantly, I have been getting to know Saskia, getting to know what I like and what I don't like, how I self-sabotage and play small, how I disconnect and distance myself to try and stay safe, how I hurt other people by shutting them out, and how I run from success and opportunities thinking they are too good to be true. I have learned that while I have many flaws, dark sides, trauma, and fears, I also have so much love, electricity, adventure, groundedness, light, resilience, and stamina.

My experience of transformation is gradual and continual. It's learning to choose to step into the unknown and allow God and those around me to surprise me and show up for me when I need it most. It's learning to lean into support when it feels uncomfortable, especially when I tell myself I don't deserve it. I wish I could tell you there is a blueprint to doing life right or to discovering and learning to fall in love with yourself, but there isn't. What I can tell you is that it starts with one step—one decision. That decision starts with saying yes to you.

MY VILLAGE

You will have great, amazing, exhilarating days, and you will have soul-wrenching, mentally exhausting days. It is so imperative that you learn to open yourself to others, be vulnerable and ask for support. I've done the whole "I've got this" I don't need anybody, and while I did survive and cope, I wasn't living—I was surviving. It became exhausting, lonely, and disempowering.

Healing takes patience, compassion, and nurturing. For me to really begin healing, I had to be willing to go back to those painful moments and feel the emotions. Everyone heals differently. For me, healing looked like going back and processing the grief and pain. Healing was opening "Pandora's box", not having a clue what would come out or how it would come out. Before I could open the box, though, I created a support system. A group of people I knew I could turn back to and rely on if I got to a low point again. This time, I wasn't going to suffer in silence.

If there was a secret to this self-love journey I could share with you, it's this: I am not doing it alone. I am not who I am today without my village. To say that I am able to live a life that is authentic to me without acknowledging those that have supported me and stood for and with me to be able to create it would be unfathomable. When I moved to NYC post-college graduation to begin a new life, I was faced with many challenges, especially when I began writing my story. My story is incomplete without my village.

8

I AM BECAUSE HE IS

*P*ost college graduation, I got offered a job in New York City. I had visited New York a couple of times before but had never envisioned or imagined moving to NYC. When I got the job offer during Covid, I was excited to have this opportunity. I was ready to begin a new life in NYC as a young adult. It would be the first time in my life that I would be paying rent and my bills myself. I was also anxious, wondering if I would be able to thrive and adapt in New York. Nonetheless, I accepted the job offer and moved to New York in August of 2020. It was challenging at first.

Being away from my family and friends and adjusting to a completely foreign lifestyle and environment, I learned to ask myself questions like "What support do I need right now" "What does support look like for me?" "What does my inner child need right now?" "What is my inner child avoiding?" Those questions supported me a lot, especially as I was attempting to create a social life during a pandemic. Indoor sitting wasn't allowed when I moved, and most restaurants, bars, and establishments closed at 10 PM.

That time alone from the rest of the world allowed me to relook at my friendships, goals, dreams, and fears and what was getting in my way of having the things I said I wanted in my life, like love. I started to call or text my friends and family more often. I started to notice the things that I actually liked for myself when no one else was around, like dancing and singing around the apartment in my underwear as I cooked dinner. So I began to play music every time I cooked and danced like no one was watching. I would even share some of those moments with my friends using social media.

I discovered that mustard yellow is my favorite color and Thainese food is one of my favorite types of food. I started doing yoga and realized I loved it a lot more than the intense fitness training I used to do. Yoga brought me peace, clarity and I felt centered after a class. I began to create content to post on my social media for my life coaching business. I slowly took on the task of doing one thing that fueled me every day. It didn't matter how big or small the thing was, as long as I made sure I did it. I started to fill my days with things that elevated and nourished me. Some days that looked like sleeping in until 4 PM and binge-watching a show on Netflix. Other days, that looked like going up to Connecticut to spend the weekend with my best friend. Sometimes it even looked like eating a piece of dark chocolate when I got home.

I began to create a self-love practice that I hadn't originally planned on. When I had a challenging week at work or in general, I would buy myself flowers, order delicious food and dessert, start a bubble bath, light a candle, put on some country or singer/songwriter music, and I would drink red or white wine (depending on my mood) while eating some dark chocolate. When the food would get there, I would find a great movie or show to watch, or I would put on the Hallmark channel and snuggle into bed, eating my food and watching TV. Those nights were some of the most rejuvenating because I was taking care of myself. I was taking the time to give myself what I desired and needed. It felt liberating.

In the journey of figuring out what supported me, fueled me, and nourished me, I started writing a manuscript.

FIRST ATTEMPT

I had a set schedule; every night from 9-11 PM, I was going to write a minimum of five pages. The goal was to be done with my manuscript in thirty days. As I began to write the first draft of my memoir, old wounds, scars, and pain resurfaced. The more I wrote about certain stories, the more I found myself sinking deeper and deeper into those stories as if they were currently happening. Some nights I was crying so much, I couldn't write and had banging headaches. Other nights, I was so excited to write about a certain story, I couldn't stop smiling, laughing, and writing. It was a rollercoaster of emotion. What felt taxing was becoming aware of old wounds that needed to be healed but not feeling ready to go back there. I began to relive what it felt like when my dad was arrested, when I first lost my virginity, when I took those pills, and all that unfolded afterward.

I had convinced myself that since it already happened and I had "gone through" it that the emotions were gone, but as I wrote those stories, they were as present as ever. My inner child was wounded and crying out to be loved and forgiven.

Some nights, when the emotions got overwhelming, I would close my eyes, envision the woman I am today, going back to those moments, sitting next to the little girl I was in those situations, and I would picture the woman I am today hugging that little girl. I would tell her, "I see you. I'm sorry. Please forgive me. Thank you. I love you." It's quite similar to the Hawai'ian Ho'pono'pono prayer: "I'm sorry. Please forgive me. Thank you. I love you." Except I added my little twist to it, "I see you." It was important to me to tell that girl I was back then that I saw her because for so long, I had felt invisible.

Some nights, I would watch old Elevation Church sermons on YouTube. Elevation Church is a non-denominational Christian Church led by Pastor Steven Furtick and Pastor Holly Furtick. Whenever I felt I needed an extra push or support, I would pick a random video, and without exception, the sermon was always exactly what I needed to hear every single time. I would walk away from those sermons feeling nourished, fueled, and ready to take on any challenges that came my way. I began to watch the sermons on most Sundays. Sometimes I would remember, and other times I would get lost in the mundane everyday life and forget about going to church. I was slowly getting back into my faith, but I was afraid of committing and being all in, so I was one foot in and one foot out.

MAY 11TH, 2021, AWAKENING

On May 11th, as I was walking home from work, a good friend of mine from my college Catholic bible study called me to inform me that a friend of ours from our bible study had passed away. She had been battling mental health and left us. As I heard the news, I was so confused. I had a million questions. I couldn't understand. When I think of her, I remember a girl who was always on top of her game at work, school, life and had one of the strongest faiths I knew. She was always talking to me about Mary (the mother of Jesus) and trying to make me understand why and how she played such an important role in the Catholic Church. Even when I didn't understand or agree with her reasoning, she never wavered and changed her ground. She stood by her word and faith and kept on sharing her love for Mary. Until this day, I can't say I understand Mary much, but I did respect my friend for standing her ground for what she believed. Whenever I had questions, I knew she was a great person to ask. So when my friend called me to let me know she had passed, I couldn't make sense of it. How? Why? What happened?

Those are questions I will never get the answer to, but as I began to ask them, I realized there was only one place I could find somewhat solace with or without the answers, God. Every day, two of my friends from Bible study and I would FaceTime to check in on one another and see how we were holding up. We would also pray the rosary for her soul every day. Even though I don't pray the rosary or quite understand it, when the girls suggested we pray it for her soul, I instantly knew that it was what she would have wanted us to do for her. We may not have been able to do anything else but at least that we could do. While those check-in and prayer calls were extremely supportive, I had so much anger and questions. I needed to talk to the big guy.

One evening, I was so angry and frustrated, I googled the nearest church and walked there. When I got there, I sat in the empty pew and began to talk angrily to God. I couldn't understand how someone who had inspired me to have more faith could have lost all faith. I couldn't understand how I didn't see it coming. I couldn't understand how I never saw the signs. As I was alone, I began to express my frustrations out loud. After minutes of expressing my anger and having my "frustration fits", I stopped and began to sob. Who I was actually mad at was not God but myself. I was mad that I wasn't a better friend. I was mad that when we last spoke, we said we would catch up but never did. I was mad that my friend was in pain, and I wasn't even able to help. I kept beating myself up: "Saskia, you're a coach, you're supposed to be able to see these things. You should've noticed."

I left church feeling empty and sad. I was filled with grief, disappointment, and melancholy. My dad called me to check up on me as I had told my family about her passing, and I told him how frustrated I was with myself for not seeing it, and he responded something that downright shook me. He said, "Saskia, remember your story, we had no idea you had gone through such difficult things, and yet we spoke to you almost every day," and at that moment, I understood.

There was nothing I could have done differently because I would have never known. If she had wanted me to know, she would have told me or shown me. But just like I was exceptional at hiding my pain and living in my shadow, so was she. That night, I went to bed, understanding that she and I were more similar than I ever knew. Our relationship was based on what we wanted one another to see. We both kept the parts of ourselves we were ashamed of hidden, and we used our smiles as our masks.

Ami, you have been one of my greatest teachers. Through your passing, I have learned that I don't want to continue rejecting support. I don't want to continue living half of a life. I don't want to keep living in the shadows. I want the world to see me. I want to share my story and my truth because I don't ever want another girl or woman like us ever to do it alone again. I know I may not get to tell all of them, but I damn sure will try.

A week after that discernment, I attended a workshop hosted by Sandra Rodriguez Bicknell that was centered around rewriting your story and finding your voice. It was exactly what I needed after feeling stuck for months since writing my first manuscript. Never in a million years did I expect that workshop to bring me such clarity on what was next for my book journey. After the workshop, we got on a call, I told her I was ready to write again, and we began to dive in. It was divine timing.

I restarted writing this book from scratch because while the first manuscript was great, it had no purpose, message, or visions. The story I tell myself is that the first manuscript was what I needed to write to realize that I had more to heal. It was what I needed to write to recognize my story and own it. It was the way I was ready to share my story with my family.

> *"If you want to go fast, go alone. If you want to go far, go together."*
>
> *-African Proverb*

During the Mid-summer of 2021, I had to move out of NYC. It wasn't something I had wanted or necessarily expected, but my visa no longer allowed me to stay, so I had to go back home. When I first left, I was very positive about the move, telling myself that it was happening for the best and that now I would have the opportunity I dreamed of, which was being a full-time coach and building my practice. It would also mean that I would finally make time for writing again. I kept on going, going and going, until I broke down a month later. The stress, anxiety, and sorrow of the move had caught up to me. It was time to allow myself to feel all of it; leaving the life I had created for myself, the man I had begun to fall in love with, the connections I had created, and the second home I had created for myself.

However, it wasn't until I left NYC that I began to feel and learn that it was okay for me to heal and go back to those memories. I felt more ready because I knew I had a support system, a village I could reach out to if I needed them. I just wasn't sure how to.

At first, I decided to take some time off social media and dive deeper into Saskia. I was doing it alone for about two weeks when I realized nothing was going to change if I kept going this way. I was anxious, depressed, and isolating myself. Therefore, I decided to do what I would in the past resist or turn away from, and I leaned into support. I had no idea what support looked like for me in this time of sorrow and grief, so I asked my coaching team to support me in figuring out what supported me. They encouraged me to practice doing the thing I was avoiding.

So, I did. I looked and asked friends around for therapist referrals, and after a couple of days, I found one I really connected with and hired her. I also started to practice asking AND receiving support from my village. I redefined what support meant to me and the way I thought it should look like. Sometimes, support looked like a pep talk from a friend or fellow coach when I questioned why I was a coach or why I was writing my book. Sometimes, it looked like taking the day off to recharge and fuel myself by silencing my phone, spending time with family, going for a run, making a delicious smoothie, and watching television with my grandma. Other times, it looked like showing up to my power-hour business bootcamp call when I didn't want to because I knew not showing up was my way of sabotaging myself and my business. I was beginning to practice doing the things I didn't want to do so that I could have the results I did want. I embraced that there isn't one way that support has to be or look like. It can look a variety of ways, but the most important thing to understand about support is that it should leave you feeling fueled, seen, acknowledged, and at ease and if it doesn't, then continue practicing.Like growth and healing, it's a process, and simply the fact that you are practicing is a huge first step

EUREKA!

As I began to dive deeper into the present moment and myself, I realized that what I had been searching for all along was always within me and around me. The love I was looking for was within me, and I was surrounded by love if only I allowed myself to receive it. The more I leaned into that love, the more I was able to attract it in my space. The more I accepted myself, the more confident I felt and the more daring I allowed myself to be. And while I was rediscovering Saskia and her village, something was still missing. As I spoke to my little sister, she reflected that what was missing in my life, especially in these moments of sorrow and grief, was faith. Faith in God, faith in a higher power.

I had learned to grow, heal and depend on myself for so long that I had forgotten about faith and God. It was either all Him or all me. I didn't know how to have faith and trust in Him without feeling powerless and weak. I had forgotten the many times he had been my strength, arms, and legs when I couldn't be for myself. I had forgotten that He was the only one that brought me peace and solace when my friend passed. He was the one that carried me through when I felt I couldn't keep going. He had been there every step of the way, supporting me even when I rejected Him over and over again. For so long, I had believed that God was against me and that He was punishing me for not following His ways. Then, after some deep reflection and introspection, I realized that if God was who I thought He was: loving, omnipotent, omnipresent, and all-powerful, then why would he ever want me to experience pain, suffering, loss, and scarcity?

It was easy for me to see that when things got very challenging and dark in my life, He wasn't there or He had caused it, but when I choose to really look back, I notice the people and things He sent my way to ensure that I wasn't utterly alone. When I was lost, scared, and lifeless, He sent me to Hawai'i to experience a whole new way of living. When I took those pills, He didn't let me die. When I rejected Him as my source of healing, He sent my cousin my way to enroll me in the transformational training. When I was having my panic attack, He had my neighbor message me and ask me if I was okay. When my dad was arrested, and I had to give my speech, He gave me the strength I needed to do it with grace and ease. The more I look back, the more I realize that He had been there every step of the way, especially when I felt the loneliest.

The way I choose to see it now is that when I wasn't willing or ready to listen to Him, He sent people and experiences my way that He knew I would listen to and learn from. He met me where I was, whatever it looked like, and every time I would restart praying, it never felt like I was being judged or rejected. It actually felt like I had never left, like He had been waiting for me all this time.

The perception of receiving the love, forgiveness, compassion, abundance, and blessings the maker of the Universe has for me was unfathomable and scary. I never felt I was good enough or I deserved it. Now, having worked with various coaches and participated in transformational trainings, I understand that the work begins with me, but I can do nothing if I keep on choosing to believe that the maker of the Universe is against me.

I'm not sure what you do or do not believe in, but I'll say it for you this way: similarly to the Law of Attraction, positive or negative thoughts bring positive or negative experiences in someone's life. So if I continue to choose to believe and tell myself that my higher power is working against me, I will continue to have that experience in my life. Things will keep happening that will prove that story right.

Now, I'm not saying that story will change overnight, but what I am offering you here is a chance to decide the story you want to keep telling yourself because God does want the best for you. He wants you to experience joy, love, peace, healing, forgiveness, friendship, connection, trust, safety, abundance, and health. The question for you is, are you ready to allow Him to lead you?

I am still working on my faith. I don't have it all figured out, and most of the time, I have no idea if I am praying right or doing "faith" right, but I continue to show up because I'm tired of running the narrative that 1) I have to do it all alone and 2) God is working against me. It hasn't worked for me in the past, and it sure as heck won't work in the future, so I am choosing to believe that 1) getting supported and held takes vulnerability and courage, it's the exact opposite of weak, and 2) God is always working everything out for my good, especially the darkest moments of my life. He is present.

HE WAS THE PIECE I WAS MISSING

While I believe that He is in control of my life, I also know that it is up to me to put in the necessary work to see the results I want for myself. He will open the doors, but I am the one that is going to have to step through. He will lead the way, but I am the one who will ultimately have to choose which path or road I want to take. He is always going to be there, one step ahead of me, guiding and paving the way, and all I get to do now is practice listening, trusting, and believing that what is planned for my life is greater than what I am currently seeing.

Just like He wants me to live into my full power, authenticity, and freedom, He also wants that for you. Lean in.

Over the past three years, I've learned that each and every single one of us has stories, fears, pasts, and secrets we keep. We all have things we hide. I was scared to share with the world out of fear of being rejected and judged. We may not share the same stories, challenges, and struggles, but we have all lived in the shadows of ourselves, another human being, or something like our job, family, society, or religion.

Fear had me living in the shadows for years, and now, faith has me living in my power and truth. Living into my truth had me join Accomplishment Coaching, where I trained for a year to become the coach I am today. Living into my truth had me give love another chance when I was terrified I would be destroyed by it. Living into my trust had me experience forgiveness and acceptance of my entire being.

Vulnerability, forgiveness, trust, and faith are probably the most terrifying things for me to lean into, but every day I choose to step into one of them. I have so much to experience and learn about this life and the world. I'm sure I will have more challenges, heartaches, and confusion, and I still get anxious and depressed, but when I do now, I lean into my village. My village keeps me going when I can't, they hold me when I fall down, and they remind me of who I am when I forget. My village is comprised of God, my family, my life coach and book coach, my therapist, and my friends that I feel have become my second home. Each and every single one of those individuals plays such a different role in my life, and each is just as necessary and instrumental. They see me, they hear me, they love me, and they stand with me every step of the journey. All I have to do is ask and receive. Most of the time, the hardest part is receiving the support I asked for.

When you want to run away from the world, hide your pain and sorrows, keep pushing while running on empty, I invite you to stop and practice something different. Practice facing the thing you are running away from. Run towards the arms of someone or people who deeply care for you. You don't need to know what you are going to say or what you are going to do in the long run. All you need to do is take that first step that you've been avoiding.

You also DO NOT have to go through this journey alone. God is right here, AND your village is waiting for you to remove that mask and lean in for support. They want to see you, not the you you pretend to be but the authentic version of who you truly are, with all of your flaws, fears, mess, and all. And if you experience rejection, know this, they are not who you want in your village because your village contains the people in your life who will see you, hear you and stick by you through the mess, confusion, and breakdowns. Don't despair if you don't build that village right away. It takes time, patience, and continual practice, especially when you want to give up. It may even require you to heal old relationships, apologize, forgive and ask for forgiveness, as well as have difficult and uncomfortable conversations.

You are worthy of being seen, loved, and accepted for who you are. You are precious, you are loved, and you are enough. YOU HAVE ALWAYS BEEN ENOUGH. God is waiting for you to lean in so He can shower you with love, support, and abundance.

9

AS IS

For so long, I thought that life was about getting to the next thing, the next level, the next goal, and as I stop and look at life, I've realized that it's actually about the here and now. We can't go back to the past, and we can't go to the future, so the present is what is available to us. Hear me out, this doesn't mean have no visions, goals, or plans. What I'm saying here is that in order to create that future and life you dream and desire, it's going to require being present in this moment, right here, right now.

As a transformational, and leadership coach, my job is to have conversations with people about their future and what they want to generate in their lives. I've discovered that through that search and journey, what occurs is a profound discovery of self. An encounter with the deepest parts of ourselves, where we get to really know who we are, what matters to us, what gets in our way, and what we truly want, not from a place of lack or need but from a place of wholeness and possibility. And that profound discovery of self only occurs in the here and now. Being so connected to oneself and the present moment that nothing else could be created but that vision and purpose.

You may be wondering what it looks like to be connected to oneself. Here's the thing, your process of connection to self will look very differently than mine, and that's perfectly okay. In my self-discovery and self-love process, I've learned that in order to deeply connect with myself, it required: vulnerability, the courage to look, acceptance of my story, especially the ones I find shameful, a ton of support, resilience, and stamina. Now, these were not built in one day or one month of practice, it took time and discipline. The matter of fact is I am still working on each of them as I am writing this. I am far from having it all figured out, and I am far from knowing it all. Just like you, I am learning, growing, and healing. The process of transformation and growth is a process of a lifetime. In my experience, I've realized that every time I thought I had mastered it or overcame it or surpassed it, there was still more for me to learn.

I'm not saying this to discourage you, but for you to know that it is okay if you find yourself falling into the same old patterns, it is okay if you thought you outgrew something and realize you haven't because it's a process. The first step of any journey or process is awareness. Being aware of the pattern and being aware that you haven't overcome it. Once you are aware, then you are in a new space where you can decide what you want to do about it. You now have the power to decide if you want to stay in that pattern or if you want to practice something different, you are now at choice. And hey, it's not always easy to practice something different. It's a whole lot easier to keep doing what you've been doing because 1) it's comfortable and 2) it's your automatic, it's what you're used to. If you do choose to want to change or shift your response to something in your life, it's going to require you really wanting it and you getting supported along the way. Support may look like hiring a coach and/or a therapist, talking to a pastor, getting a mentor, joining a mastermind program, getting sober or any other structure that is related to what it is you want to accomplish in your life. If you want to experience something you've never experienced before, it will require you trying something you've never tried before.

You're going to need to create a why or a what for that is big enough to withstand the breakdowns and setbacks that will occur. Whenever I've stepped out of my comfort zone, as I've mentioned throughout my story, I always experienced setbacks and breakdowns. The thing that had me keep showing up, which had me continue when I wanted to quit, was my why, the bigger picture, and the vision behind what I was doing. When the vision is greater than the pain, hardship, and breakdowns, you will keep showing up, but it will require resilience and stamina. It will require practice, practice, practice. It will require you to continue to show up in the arena when you want to give up. It will require you to step out of your comfort zone every single time. It will require faith in your vision and support to keep you going.

IT WAS ALWAYS ABOUT YOU

Here's the thing, everything I mentioned doesn't require you to be anybody else but YOU. There is nothing you need to reach, be or do to be enough. As is, is all you need. YOU already have all you need and possess to tap into that vulnerability, resilience, stamina, love, and vision. All you get to do is be you fully, and in that practice of fully being yourself "as is", vulnerability, resilience, stamina, asking, and receiving support will come with time. Because the more you are able to be with yourself, the more you will open up to your faith, family, loved ones, and the world as yourself. The more you open up, the more your truth will come out, and the more you will get to experience. That profound discovery and connection of self happens in the as is, nowhere else, because everywhere else is performance, pretending, doing and none of it is actually about you being present to you, your emotions, your fears, your concerns, your greatness, your voice, and your beauty.

And know this: whenever you feel that your story, past, traumas, and voice are too much for a space, consider that space is too small for you. It's just not the space for you, because any space that is too small isn't yours. There is absolutely nothing wrong with being you. So if it doesn't fit, it's not yours. And why want something that keeps you small when you can have an array of things that hold and support your greatness.

You are made by the King of the universe, and you were created to be GREAT. Every single person, no matter what path they choose, who they are, or what they do for a living, they were put here in this lifetime, on this planet for a purpose.

You weren't created by accident even if you were told you were—you were created for a bigger purpose and vision. Your story is your testimony. Your story is your weapon. Your story is the door opener in your life. Your story is your power, not your weakness. Next time someone tells you— "you're not enough"—"you don't matter"—"you're not capable"—"you're unworthy"—"you're a mistake"—"you're a waste"—remember that they didn't create you, they didn't give you your purpose or vision, they are probably reflecting how they feel about themselves, and they do not hold the pen to your life.

YOU are the author of your life. YOU get to choose which story you will write. YOU are at choice. YOU have the power. YOU are and have always been enough. YOU weren't made by mistake—God doesn't make mistakes. YOU are exactly who you are meant to be because there is NO ONE else that can think, feel, be and do it like you. There is only YOU, and there is a very specific reason for that. Don't you ever forget that there is only one you for a reason. Only you can accomplish what you were created here to create. The vision, the dreams, the goals, and plans were all instilled in YOU for a reason. You may think your vision is similar to others, but if you take a closer look, you'll realize no one sees it like you, which is why only you can create it.

Now the choice is up to you. What will you choose to do with your story? What's the story you'll choose to tell?

10

ABOUT THE AUTHOR

*S*askia St Lot is a transformational and leadership coach who was born and raised in Port-au-Prince, Haiti. She moved to the United States of America to study Public Health at the University of Miami, where she graduated with a Bachelor of Science along with minors in psychology, management, and dance. Post-graduation, she pursued her interest in Public Health by moving to New York City, where she worked as an Account Manager and Marketer for a homecare agency for about a year.

She then pursued her passion and graduated from a a one-year coaching training program, Accomplishment Coaching. She will be getting her International Coach Federation (ICF) Professional Coaching Certification (PCC) in the summer of 2022, where she will be recognized globally as an accredited ICF coach.

She is also a motivational speaker and now a published author. She is a radical self-love advocate and campaigner, and she is 23-years-old. Connection is her life purpose, and her vision for the world is one that is connected, authentic, loving, and expressive.

11

REDISCOVER WITH SASKIA ST LOT

I am a woman, daughter, friend, coach, and motivational speaker committed to promoting self-love and rediscovery of self. Through my coaching sessions, I support women in rediscovering themselves, their calling, purpose and create a once and for all shift in their lives. I stand for authenticity, freedom, abundance, and expression. If you are ready to begin your self-discovery journey where you will rediscover your essence and step into the woman you were created to be, this is your calling. This is the moment where you get to decide what you want for yourself. Through coaching, you will experience:

1. Accountability & Support
2. Radical self-love & Forgiveness
3. Life purpose & Passion
4. Resilience & Stamina
5. Clarity & Peace
6. Project design & Abundance

You will rediscover who you are, what you are capable of, and what you can create in your life when you choose to step into who you've always been at your core. You will begin to live a life designed by YOU.

Website: www.saskiastlot.com
Instagram Handle: Saskia_stlot
Email: Saskia.stlot@accomplishmentcoaching.com

Made in the USA
Middletown, DE
11 November 2023